THE MANIFESTO FOR TEACHING ONLINE

THE MANIFESTO FOR TEACHING ONLINE

SIÂN BAYNE, PETER EVANS, RORY EWINS,
JEREMY KNOX, JAMES LAMB, HAMISH
MACLEOD, CLARA O'SHEA, JEN ROSS,
PHILIPPA SHEAIL, AND CHRISTINE SINCLAIR

ILLUSTRATED BY KIRSTY JOHNSTON

THE MIT PRESS   CAMBRIDGE, MASSACHUSETTS   LONDON, ENGLAND

This book was set in ITC Stone and Avenir by New Best-set Typesetters Ltd. Printed and bound in the United States of America.

Library of Congress Cataloging-in-Publication Data

Names: Bayne, Siân, author.
Title: The manifesto for teaching online / Siân Bayne, Peter Evans, Rory Ewins, Jeremy Knox, James Lamb, Hamish Macleod, Clara O'Shea, Jen Ross, Philippa Sheail, Christine Sinclair ; illustrated by Kirsty Johnston.
Description: Cambridge, Massachusetts : The MIT Press, 2020. | Includes bibliographical references and index.
Identifiers: LCCN 2020002988 | ISBN 9780262539838 (paperback)
Subjects: LCSH: Internet in higher education. | Web-based instruction. | Education, Higher—Computer-assisted instruction.
Classification: LCC LB2395.7 .B39 2020 | DDC 378.1/7344678—dc23
LC record available at https://lccn.loc.gov/2020002988

10 9 8 7 6 5 4 3 2 1

This book is dedicated to all the students on the Edinburgh MSc in Digital Education past, present, and future: thank you for all your boldness, generosity, insight and trust.

CONTENTS

THE 2016 MANIFESTO FOR TEACHING ONLINE

Online can be the privileged mode. Distance is a positive principle, not a deficit.

Place is differently, not less, important online.

Text has been troubled: many modes matter in representing academic knowledge.

We should attend to the materialities of digital education. The social isn't the whole story.

Openness is neither neutral nor natural: it creates and depends on closures.

Can we stop talking about digital natives?

Digital education reshapes its subjects. The possibility of the "online version" is overstated.

There are many ways to get it right online. "Best practice" neglects context.

Distance is temporal, affective, political: not simply spatial.

Aesthetics matter: interface design shapes learning.

Massiveness is more than learning at scale: it also brings complexity and diversity.

Online teaching need not be complicit with the instrumentalization of education.

A digital assignment can live on. It can be iterative, public,
risky, and multivoiced.

Remixing digital content redefines authorship.

Contact works in multiple ways. Face time is overvalued.

Online teaching should not be downgraded to "facilitation."

Assessment is an act of interpretation, not just measurement.

Algorithms and analytics recode education: pay attention!

A routine of plagiarism detection structures-in distrust.

Online courses are prone to cultures of surveillance. Visibility
is a pedagogical and ethical issue.

Automation need not impoverish education: we welcome our
new robot colleagues.

Don't succumb to campus envy: we are the campus.

INTRODUCTION: WE ARE THE CAMPUS

[A manifesto makes] explicit (that is, manifest) a subtle but radical transformation in the definition of what it means to progress, that is, to process forward and meet new prospects. Not as a war cry for an avant-garde to move even further and faster ahead, but rather as a warning, a call to attention, so as to stop going further in the same way as before toward the future. (Latour 2010, 473)

Teaching as a team is common in higher education, and perhaps works particularly well in programs strongly driven by the research of those doing the teaching. Students and teachers benefit from bringing multiple, entangled perspectives to the task of making sense of the world, where those perspectives are informed and energized by good research and scholarship. However, it is relatively rare for large teaching teams to come together to define and agree on a shared political and pedagogical stance on the act of teaching. Reaching such an agreement

Figure 0.1

takes a lot of time, commitment, creativity, negotiation, and open dialogue among people who do not always entirely agree with each other's stance and methods even though they share a mutual respect.

The Manifesto for Teaching Online emerged from this context of team teaching and negotiation. Its authors are all researchers at the Centre for Research in Digital Education at the University of Edinburgh, and we are all teachers on the fully online master's program in digital education, offered by the School of Education since 2006. We first published the manifesto in its original postcard form in 2011, then again

Manifesto for Teaching Online ✳ Distance is a positive principle, not a deficit. Online can be the privileged mode. ✳ The possibility of the 'online version' is overstated. The best online courses are born digital. ✳ By redefining connection we find we can make eye contact online. ✳ 'Best practice' is a totalising term blind to context – there are many ways to get it right. ✳ Every course design is philosophy and belief in action. ✳ The aesthetics of online course design are too readily neglected: courses that are fair of (inter)face are better places to teach and learn in. ✳ Online courses are prone to cultures of surveillance: our visibility to each other is a pedagogical and ethical issue. ✳ Text is being toppled as the only mode that matters in academic writing. ✳ Visual and hypertextual representations allow arguments to emerge, rather than be stated. ✳ New forms of writing make assessors work harder: they remind us that assessment is an act of interpretation. ✳ Feedback can be digested, worked with, created from. In the absence of this, it is just 'response'. ✳ Assessment strategies can be designed to allow for the possibility of resistance. ✳ A routine of plagiarism detection structures-in a relation of distrust. ✳ Assessment is a creative crisis as much as it is a statement of knowledge. ✳ Place is differently, not less, important online. ✳ Closed online spaces limit the educational power of the network. ✳ Online spaces can be permeable and flexible, letting networks and flows replace boundaries. ✳ Course processes are held in a tension between randomness and intentionality. ✳ Online teaching should not be downgraded into 'facilitation'. ✳ Community and contact drive good online learning. ✳ Written by teachers and researchers in online education. University of Edinburgh MSc in E-learning 2011

✳ This document is intended to stimulate ideas about creative online teaching. It is written by teachers and researchers in the field of online education, and attempts to re-think some of the orthodoxies and unexamined truisms surrounding the field. The manifesto is informed by theory, research and practice, but positions itself deliberately outside the writing genres associated with these. It is the result of a research project but in its form attempts an alternative version of how we might understand research output. Each point is deliberately interpretable – the manifesto is both a contingent statement of intent and a starting point for (re)thinking what online education might be. ✳ For more about the project which generated the manifesto, please see: www.education.ed.ac.uk/swop/

Figure 0.2   The 2011 manifesto

in 2016, with a third iteration planned for 2021—a five-year rhythm that seems likely to continue into the foreseeable future. Five years is a long time in all academic fields, but particularly those that navigate the continually shifting landscape of technological change. And while our values as teachers and researchers in digital education may not shift that much, the context in which we apply them changes substantially year by year.

The manifesto emerged from a small research project, conducted between 2009 and 2011, that was funded to interrogate the online assessment and feedback methods we had developed in our program and to extend and share these with other educators. Over more than a year of intense discussion among the teaching team and work with the students who were appointed as research associates to the project, we found

Figure 0.3   The 2016 manifesto

that we had done important work in formulating and articulating a shared teaching philosophy capable of driving such a project. Sharing this with others seemed to require a more experimental and engaged approach than the usual research papers and blog articles. A rough draft of the first Manifesto for Teaching Online was written and then refined over a series of discussions and events among a wider group of students and colleagues. By 2011 we had finalized the text and worked with a designer (Oliver Brookes) on the first print version. Over the course of 2015, an expanded team of teachers on our master's program (the authors of this book) revisited and reassembled the manifesto into its 2016 version, which Oliver Brookes then redesigned.

The aim of the manifesto was partly to develop our own teaching by articulating our shared values and their political and philosophical basis. Its theme was our practice, but it was also a way of describing and building on our research. Its critical goal was to push back on two linked areas we saw, and continue to see, as damaging: (1) the impoverished techno-corporate futures for education being normalized by corporate and government "ed-tech" and (2) the orthodoxies framing traditional higher education teaching, which so often fail to properly account for digital methods.

In relation to the first of these, we wanted to find ways of resisting the instrumentalizing, ethically lax ways in which ed-tech tends to be described in the industry, political, and management spheres, a discourse focusing on technology as an inevitable "solution" to the "problems" surrounding education and educators. Here, techno-instrumentalism drives visions of a future defined by the values of corporate interest, efficiency, and productivity, rarely taking into account the values and experience of teachers and students themselves. In relation to the second, we wanted to push against the routine privileging of on-campus teaching in universities and the structural downgrading of online methods that cascade from this. We wanted to emphasize that being online opens up new, creative, highly engaged ways of teaching that deserve to be valued on their own terms. It is this point that underlies one of the key statements of the manifesto itself:

Don't succumb to campus envy: we are the campus.

During the proofing stage of this book, the COVID-19 crisis hit. Within weeks universities around the globe radically reshaped their teaching methods as on-campus students returned home, university staff locked up their offices, and communities locked down. In our own university, as in many others, all teaching shifted online within days and longer-term planning for the coming academic year became focused on how to continue to teach—and recruit—without guaranteed access to our campus teaching spaces. In this changed world, every faculty member became an online teacher, every student became a distance learner, and the very survival of some universities became entangled with their ability to manage the digital "pivot."

It will be a while before we are able to fully understand how this shift has affected educational institutions, professionals, and students long term. However, in this new world, in which fully digital teaching methods leapt from the margins to the mainstream in days, we found that the manifesto not only held up but became even more necessary, particularly in its resistance to instrumental logics and its call to be bold and critical when approaching the digital. That said, some of its meanings did shift when refracted by the lens of the pandemic. **We are the campus** was previously a call from the margins by students and teachers working in geospatially distanced networks. During the global COVID-19 lockdown it became a description of the operational mode of the majority.

One of the key manifesto points that became particularly resonant was perhaps this one: **Online can be the privileged mode. Distance is a positive principle, not a deficit.** Many of us, at the time of writing this passage, do not feel distance to be a positive principle. We miss our campuses, our offices, being co-present with our students and colleagues. We are worn out by the glitchy intensity of video meetings, by the long days on email, and by the loss of the handshake, the casual conversation, the closeness. However, we have also seen that networked distance has enabled us to build new proximities that seem likely to persist even when campuses reopen. Post-COVID there is likely to be a willingness to understand that teaching online can be creative, experimental, and connected in new and productive ways beyond the instrumental "needs must." While it of course creates new exclusions, we have seen that freedom from the requirement for physical and temporal co-presence can work to the benefit of many, much of the time. When distance once again becomes a question of choice, not a necessity, we will collectively be in a better and more informed position to understand it as a positive principle in many contexts.

This issue of context is a vital one and is embedded across the manifesto. We do not make unifying and totalizing claims around "best practice" but argue consistently that context drives our institutional and individual choices. Post-pandemic—and still having to plan for other profound crises affecting mobility such as climate change, political instability, and the likelihood of future public health crises—our context will be one in which individuals and institutions will need to do some bold thinking in relation to resilience, access, teaching quality, and inclusion. The common assumption that online is second best in all contexts will not hold.

WHY A MANIFESTO?

Committing to the production of a manifesto gave us a chance to work beyond the boundaries of the formalized and institutionalized modes of writing with which we are most familiar as academics: the academic paper or monograph, the quality assurance report, the outcomes-oriented course document. It forced us to work intensively as a team, over the period of a year in the first instance, to agree on the core points of our shared teaching philosophy and then formulate these in a way that was succinct, provocative, and engaging. As an exercise in reaching a shared understanding of what constitutes teaching quality, it surpassed to a significant degree the formalized and routinized institutional processes of quality assurance, allowing us to develop our thinking alongside our students, colleagues in other areas of the university, and a global public. It enabled us to tighten the links between our teaching and our research in a light-touch, agile way that catalyzed the academic literature in the interests of formulating and describing our practice.

The manifesto has been opened up to a global public from the start. It has been extensively blogged, remixed, reinterpreted, annotated, tweeted, contested, critiqued, keynoted, and used by colleagues across the globe who are thinking seriously about the practice of teaching in digital contexts, however it is interpreted. We have seen the manifesto postcard displayed on the walls of academic offices around the world. There are now two postcard designs, two videos (Lamb 2013, 2017), several academic papers, and translations into Chinese, Spanish, and Croatian. The Manifesto for Teaching Online is distinctive among academic manifestos in that it is not only written; it is also, in its postcard, video, and now book forms, designed. This perhaps accounts for some of its appeal and its openness to commentary and remix. What we have not produced to date, however, is an extended text that explicitly links the abbreviated, punchy statements of the manifesto to the large body of research and practice from which it emerges. That is the purpose of this book.

As a team, we see this text not so much as a book about the manifesto but as an extended manifesto in itself. Its aims are the same as those of the manifesto in its postcard and video formats: it is a call to attention, a point of pause, a distillation of a research program, and a statement of teaching values. In line with the quotation from Latour's (2010) "An Attempt at a Compositionist Manifesto," which opens this introduction, it argues not for further and faster movement into a promised future. Colonization and acceleration have not, in general, proved positive models for education. Rather, it asks us to reconsider what it means to progress, to stop going further in the same way as before, to take time to think differently. Latour refers to this as a "subtle but radical transformation in the definition of what it means to progress," suggesting that we need to rethink the conventional purpose of the manifesto as an antireactionary, revolutionary call to arms by an avant-garde committed to the ideal of progress.

Our manifesto never set out to be avant-garde: the idea of "progress," writes Latour, has become too contentious and temporality is too messy a notion to reduce to a simple forward march. Revolution itself has been reduced to an empty buzzword in education as in other areas. However, like Latour, we would hold that the idea of the manifesto still has a purpose. In our case, this is to suggest ways of thinking about digital education *made manifest* in terms other than those that have become embedded and normalized in higher education practice and policy, jolting the truisms and commonsense clichés of educational technology into some other future: one that is challenging, critical, and exciting. The manifesto is contingent, open to debate, to change, to reworking as the field itself shifts. It is a call to attention rather than a call to arms.

IN THE HANDS OF TEACHERS

One of the core ideas driving the manifesto is that good digital education lies in the hands of teachers. The dominant corporate and policy narratives currently surrounding educational technology tend to assume the inevitability of an automated, algorithmically driven, metricized, and surveillance-normalizing future in which the place of teaching practice and professionalism is often entirely sidelined by the promise of technocorporate solutions to loosely defined problems. The promises of personalization and data-driven decision-making, fueled by technorationalist instrumentalism, rarely offer teachers either a central role or a ready way in to considering how our professionalism might inform and develop with technological change in ways other than assuming a driving imperative for us to "skill up."

When the first version of the manifesto was published in 2011, we were taken to task by some commentators for calling it a manifesto for *teaching* online rather than a manifesto for *learning* online. This seemed to us to entirely miss the point: the manifesto is unapologetically about the practice and profession of teaching in higher education. The "learnification" discourse, which has had a lockdown on education in recent decades, has been complicit with the instrumentalization of education and the erasure of the teacher, as Gert Biesta (2012, 2017) has so compellingly and consistently argued. It has also amplified and consolidated ways of thinking about digital education in terms of individualized and entirely self-determined students that is often deeply unhelpful to students themselves. The manifesto starts from the position that we need to value and work with the idea of the teacher, however that role might be shifted and redefined by technological change.

So the manifesto advocates for those of us actually teaching using technology, arguing that we need to take active control and ownership of digital education, whether that means a refusal to reduce our role to that of facilitation (**Online teaching should not be downgraded to "facilitation"**), a move to actively rethink how we assess and evaluate students (**Text has been troubled: many modes matter in representing academic knowledge**), or to consider how we might remain open to reimagining automation on our own terms (**Automation need not impoverish education: we welcome our new robot colleagues.**).

IN PRACTICE

This book emphasizes the theories and research that have informed the manifesto, but it is also very much based in our practice as online teachers. We have team-taught the online master's program in digital education at the University of Edinburgh since 2006. This is a program that was set up to offer students a critical and research-led curriculum in this area at a time when much of the focus around e-learning was technical and skills driven. Several hundred students have since passed through the program, from many regions of the globe; the diversity, spread, and commitment of our student cohort have been significant to its success.

This program has also worked as a huge, vibrant playground for trying out new approaches to teaching and learning online. We have been able to be very flexible in how we have designed our teaching through several waves of technological change, from the early days of Web 2.0 and user-generated content in the mid-2000s, to riding the wave of social media as it became mainstream, using it to build our community of learners at a time when this seemed a much simpler and less troubled proposition than it now is. We adapted to the rise of YouTube and the face-time, video-link culture that emerged as bandwidths increased. We adopted teaching in virtual worlds, for several years using Second Life as one of our core teaching spaces. We developed pedagogies for mobile learning and new approaches to learning analytics that placed data in the hands of students. We ran one of the first massive open online courses in the United Kingdom (the E-learning and Digital Cultures MOOC), and developed a "teacherbot" prototype to explore what teacher-designed automation might look like. Over this same period, we developed research programs on the social topographies of distance education, open education, postcolonialism and posthumanism, the temporalities of distance learning, student network formation using social media, and much more.

It is this context of interlinked practice and research that frames the manifesto, and we have been exceptionally lucky to work with students who are motivated and driven by the same desire to experiment, take risks, and be highly creative as they learn with and through each other and the teaching team. The manifesto focuses on the practice of teaching and on teachers, but the standards these students have set for us drive our desire to teach at our best, and for this reason we dedicate this book to them.

The context of the manifesto is teaching within institutions of higher education, so much of what follows is written in relation to formal teaching within universities in particular. There is relevance to other sectors throughout, but we have not tried to homogenize sector differences and smooth them over. It would be interesting to see another group write a manifesto for digital education in K–12 schools or lifelong learning and to view together the convergences and disjunctures.

IN SUMMARY

This book is divided into five parts, within each of which we have clustered linked segments covering each of the points in the 2016 manifesto. We have tried to make each segment readable as a stand-alone entity for readers who want to dip in, though it is in part I that the underlying conceptual and theoretical rationale for these is spelled out in some detail. The book does not unfold a sequentially developing series of arguments, but like the manifesto itself, it offers a series of propositions and provocations that cluster around a core set of key theories and perspectives, all anchored by an affirmation of the value of teachers and teaching.

Part I, "Politics and Instrumental Logics," sets out the key frameworks used in the book. It explains what we mean when we discuss instrumental logics in digital education and, briefly, why theories of sociomateriality drive much of the thinking behind the manifesto. It also explains some additional terminology we have drawn on, to different extents, throughout: *learnification*, *essentialism*, and *posthumanism*. It does this while expanding on five manifesto points in which we have attempted to challenge the instrumental framing of digital technology in education—the technology-as-tool rhetoric that so regularly blocks attempts to understand digital education as social and complex:

1. We should attend to the materialities of digital education. The social isn't the whole story.
2. Can we stop talking about digital natives?
3. There are many ways to get it right online. "Best practice" neglects context.
4. Online teaching need not be complicit with the instrumentalization of education.
5. Online teaching should not be downgraded to "facilitation."

In part II, we move on to consider how technological change has opened up ways of representing academic knowledge that we believe should be more widely used in universities as we develop new, creative methods for assessing and evaluating our students' work. This part, "Beyond Words," addresses the manifesto points that tackle composition, communication, evaluation, and authorship, arguing that teaching online gives us an opportunity to rethink established understandings of originality, textual stability, and authorship itself. It introduces the theories of multimodality that have helped us develop our own practices in this area.

6. Text has been troubled: many modes matter in representing academic knowledge.
7. Aesthetics matter: interface design shapes learning.
8. Remixing digital content redefines authorship.
9. Assessment is an act of interpretation, not just measurement.
10. A digital assignment can live on. It can be iterative, public, risky, and multivoiced.

From here we move on in part III, "Recoding Education," to two connected areas of digital that have been framed in recent years as being fundamentally disruptive to higher education: (1) open education and massive open online courses (MOOCs) and (2) artificial intelligence and automation. Our stance here is that the hyperbole surrounding these has been accompanied by a neglect of the wider political, social, and educational contexts in which they are situated. We argue for greater interrogation of what we mean when we talk about openness in education, for a greater focus on the problematic ways in which education at scale tends to ignore diversity and difference in favor of a homogenized idea of the learner, and, finally, that data-driven technologies and algorithmic interventions in education have largely failed to address issues of power, agency, and teacher professionalism.

11. Openness is neither neutral nor natural: it creates and depends on closures.
12. Massiveness is more than learning at scale: it also brings complexity and diversity.
13. Algorithms and analytics recode education: pay attention!
14. Automation need not impoverish education: we welcome our new robot colleagues.

Part IV, "Face, Space, and Place," is primarily concerned with challenging the historical orthodoxy that saw, and often still sees, digital and online education as fundamentally inferior to education conducted on-campus and face-to-face. It is in this part of the book in which we most explicitly address the question of *distance* education as distinguished from *digital* education generally. We argue for seeing online education as a positive principle, not a second best. Working with this idea, however, requires us to look again at some of the terms we take for granted when we describe higher education pedagogy. We ask for a reevaluation of what we mean by *contact time* and *online version*, by what it means to be *at university* for distance students who are never in the university, and, finally, what we mean by *distance* itself. Here, we make the argument that geospatial distance is only one of the distancings we work with when we teach online distance programs.

15. Online can be the privileged mode. Distance is a positive principle, not a deficit.
16. Contact works in multiple ways. Face time is overvalued. Digital education reshapes its subjects. The possibility of the "online version" is overstated.
17. Place is differently, not less, important online.
18. Distance is temporal, affective, political: not simply spatial

Finally, part V, "Surveillance and (Dis)trust," returns to a focus on digital education in its more generic sense, arguing that surveillance is becoming routinized in higher education and that such practices have the effect of reducing, rather than increasing, the trust among students, teachers, administrators, and technologists that is essential to high-quality education. We argue that surveillance regimes and architectures in the wider society should not be uncritically replicated in colleges and universities and that teachers and the wider academic community need to push back on the creeping normalization of surveillant practices in teaching.

19. Online courses are prone to cultures of surveillance. Visibility is a pedagogical and ethical issue.
20. A routine of plagiarism detection structures-in distrust.

DON'T SUCCUMB TO CAMPUS ENVY: WE ARE THE CAMPUS

Finally, we have used this introduction to highlight one point from the manifesto that we are particularly fond of: **Don't succumb to campus envy: we are the campus.**

In our own research with online students, we found that while distance students had many ways of relating to the built campus of the university, one notable position was of campus envy—a tendency to view the campus as an emotional and symbolic home and as a kind of touchstone or guarantor of the authenticity of academic experience, without necessarily wanting to actually be physically present within it (we discuss this research in more detail in part IV). While we felt it was important to acknowledge that "the campus" has important symbolic value for students who may never visit it, we also wanted to make the point that what the campus *is* is now constituted in many different ways by people, technologies, spaces, texts, data sets, and networks coming together with a fluidity that makes the boundaries of the university itself extremely porous. This is as true for contemporary cohorts of highly mobile students attending colleges and universities in the conventional sense as it is for the growing numbers of cohorts we define as distance learners.

It is this kind of shift in thinking that we wished to prompt and advocate for as we wrote the manifesto, seeing it as a way of bursting open some of the assumptions around what constitutes quality and authenticity long taken for granted in higher education teaching, and usually revolving around the default privileging of the on-campus experience and the face-to-face encounter. We wanted to start to build our own future for digital education—one that resists these orthodoxies alongside the technodeterminist ed-tech narratives that have dominated the field to date. The Manifesto for Teaching Online is a collective piece of work that embodies a commitment to working otherwise; it blurs the distinction between research and practice, between the individuated and the collective, between the textual and the visual, being equally a statement of intent, of critique and of hope.

I

POLITICS AND
INSTRUMENTAL LOGICS

MANIFESTO POINTS COVERED

There are many ways to get it right online. "Best practice" neglects context.

We should attend to the materialities of digital education. The social isn't the whole story.

Online teaching need not be complicit with the instrumentalization of education.

Online teaching should not be downgraded to "facilitation."

Can we stop talking about digital natives?

Figure 1.1

INTRODUCTION

This part tackles five key points from the manifesto, in the process setting out some of the theoretical foundations drawn on throughout the book. First, we introduce theories of **socio-materiality**, which emphasize that teaching is a complex and highly contextual activity bringing together people, texts, images, locations, objects, technologies, and methods in many different ways. These gatherings are situated, multifaceted, emergent, and therefore unique, requiring us to question the notion of best practice and replace it with an openness to multiplicity and difference. **There are many ways to get it right online. "Best practice" neglects context.**

We then build on this in chapter 2 as we rethink the dominant assumption that human sociality and agency alone drive the practices of education. Instead, we emphasize the agencies of the materials, objects, and infrastructures that come together in the production of teaching and learning. In this way, we briefly introduce theories of **posthumanism** and make this argument: **We should attend to the materialities of digital education. The social isn't the whole story**.

Digital education is often perceived as being complicit with the reproduction of the **instrumental logics** of neoliberalism and commodification within education. In chapter 3, we make an assertion that is central to the message of the manifesto: **Online teaching need not be complicit with the instrumentalization of education**. We argue that understanding digital education as critical and sociomaterial opens up new, and better, ways of understanding and practicing online teaching.

We then extend these ideas into a discussion in chapter 4 of the role of the teacher online, arguing that reductive understandings of the "teacher function"—those that see digital technologies as unproblematically enabling the automation, scaling, and acceleration of education—converge with "**learnification**" (Biesta 2012) to deprofessionalize teaching. They underemphasize the role of the teacher as subject expert and critical practitioner by describing the core skill of the online teacher as facilitation. We argue that this reduces teaching to a level where it can be conducted by automated agents or unproblematically delivered by an underpaid, undervalued academic precariat. **Online teaching should not be downgraded to "facilitation."**

Finally, in chapter 5, we continue the consideration of how we value the teacher by tackling the idea of the digital native— one of the terms that has been most damagingly formative for digital education and continues to persist. We argue that this is an essentializing term that is problematic for the way in which it normalizes colonialist metaphors and has historically worked to devalue the professionalism of the teacher. **Can we stop talking about digital natives?**

1

THERE ARE MANY WAYS TO GET IT RIGHT ONLINE. "BEST PRACTICE" NEGLECTS CONTEXT.

Our manifesto celebrates multiple ways of teaching online. As this book pulls together aspects of the research that has shaped digital education over the past decade, it also works at times as an extended reflection on ten years of a specific teaching program, the master's in digital education at the University of Edinburgh. This program asks students to work across and through a plethora of environments, modes, methods, and agents for teaching and learning. Environments include the traditional learning management system or virtual learning environment, discussion boards, blogging and microblogging, live chat events, video tutorials, virtual worlds, massive multiplayer games, shared documents for editing, shared spaces for playing with data, visualization apps, video, MOOCs, podcasts and many more. This abundance of digital environments is mirrored in a diversity of pedagogical approaches and teaching methods, including peer learning, tutoring one-to-one, problem-based learning, experiential learning, dialogue, multimodal assessment design, prototyping, dialogue, and games.

Furthermore, students—and this is common to many other online programs—come from across the United Kingdom and continental Europe, North and South America, Australia, the Middle East, Africa, and Asia. Almost all of our students are mid- (or later) career professionals—whether academics, learning technologists, consultants, teachers, or corporate learning and development practitioners. Our students bring with them their jobs and careers, families, troubles, networks, and knowledge, enriching the program and their peers with the complexity and pattern of their lives.

Reflecting the disciplinary multiplicities of digital education, the teaching team on this particular program themselves work from various backgrounds, including languages and literature, psychology, physics, political science, information sciences, cultural studies, sociology, and computer science. This disciplinary diversity is further enhanced by work with guest teachers from around the world, drawing on the open digital networks that the teaching team, colleagues, and students are engaged in.

Building on this rich complexity—the context of our work as teachers—we challenge the notion of teaching as being necessarily focused on preexisting "objects" of study, or on students as stable "learning" subjects. Rather, we understand teaching, learning, and assessment as emergent, performed through dynamic entanglements of both social and material components—people, objects, discourses, texts. These entanglements create multiple, coexisting realities of understanding (Law 2004). Teaching and learning are understood in this context as processes of assembling and gathering of people, digital technologies, curricula, work and study spaces, and artifacts of assessment (Fenwick and Edwards 2010), which both consolidate and resist existing relations of power (Boys 2016). For those of us authoring the manifesto, this perspective offers a way to open digital teaching to difference, making—through its multiplicity—space to challenge orthodoxies (such as "best practice") that homogenize and reduce it.

This perspective on digital education takes us beyond transactional concerns with students' ease of access to materials, expertise, or qualifications, toward understanding digital education as a collective, emergent, political endeavor achieved in specific contexts involving very different arrays of pedagogies, people, and technologies. Teaching involves navigating this complexity to enable autonomous thinking within the particular institutional contexts of formal education and within the particular educational processes of a specific program of study. Teaching is therefore enacted within specific networks and is situationally contingent and inherently multiple. With such a view, the very idea of a single, immutable best practice becomes untenable: online and offline, there are many ways to get it right.

Snapshot

Our MSc in digital education program uses many different digital environments to help students experience the possibilities and limitations of multiple platforms. For real-time discussion and debate, we have tried over the years to work within virtual environments that turn away from the flat spaces of videoconferencing environments, which tend to replicate classroom practice in their foregrounding of content and teacher over student participation. We have often chosen to use spaces that students can actively build and playfully inhabit in new ways that move beyond classroom metaphors.

One example was our use for many years of the virtual world of Linden Lab's *Second Life* within a university-owned space we built called Holyrood Park. Here, teaching practices were made physical in circular seating patterns. There were no screens or blackboards; the space was designed and built to nurture discussion and playful representation of self through avatars (for more, see O'Shea and Dozier 2014; Sheail 2015). Many students enjoyed this virtual world as an immersive and fun space, in which learning could take place on beaches or around campfires and students could spend time together talking in gardens or platforms in the sky. However, a sizable number of students found this virtual world challenging and hard work: user interfaces were unintuitive, navigation opaque, and the act of building virtual objects and spaces complex and difficult. Sometimes avatars would not render correctly and behaved erratically, or nonstudents and occasional trolls would appear to disturb teaching sessions. What was a successful and engaging learning environment for some was clearly not for others. Ultimately we abandoned *Second Life* because the effects of this particular assemblage of people and practices was limiting the learning being achieved and students began to perceive the platform itself as outdated.

Our students now explore playful spatial configurations in digital education in *Minecraft*, the sandbox game and open world developed by Mojang and now owned by Microsoft. *Minecraft* is not a replacement for *Second Life*; rather, it is an alternative assemblage with a specific purpose: to function as an environment for students to build and develop new reflections on digital teaching space. The sociability of *Second Life* is to a large extent removed in this environment, though the ability for individual students to build and make is much enhanced, and students are able to visit one another's work in a single digital landscape. Some students love this; others find it opaque to use and frustrating to craft.

For us, these two examples emphasize that teaching is a matter of continual negotiation and adaptation of the various configurations of technology, people, trends, learning aims, and dynamics available to us. The richness and variety of the choices of space open to us when we teach online emphasizes this, though it is of course also true for physically co-present teaching. We see good teaching and learning as an exercise in continual recrafting, not an adherence to entrenched notions of good practice. What works in *Second Life* will not in *Minecraft*, or in a physically embodied classroom, or in a WhatsApp discussion, or in a lab.

For us, education has the purpose of developing within students the techniques and aptitudes of critical reasoning within broader ethical frameworks that promote the common good. It involves exploring potential social and material reconfigurations of practices to generate ethical outcomes by including that which has been excluded or oppressed (van der Velden 2009), developing alternative, and we hope better, realities. The practices of critique within our own master's in digital education involve recognizing and contesting common assumptions about the relations among educational institutions, staff, students, and digital technologies. In particular, we challenge the dominant framings of digital education that assume technology naturally empowers users to practice better learning, or necessarily enables institutions to create more effective or efficient ways of teaching (Bayne 2016). We argue that these instrumental framings consolidate existing relations of power (Boys 2016) and prevent us from building alternative futures for digital education that resist its instrumentalization. **There are many ways to get it right online. "Best practice" neglects context.**

2

WE SHOULD ATTEND TO THE MATERIALITIES OF DIGITAL EDUCATION. THE SOCIAL ISN'T THE WHOLE STORY.

Higher education is often understood in terms of a materiality anchored in Matthew Arnold's "dreaming spires" and iconic architectural statements, lecture halls, libraries, offices, and meeting rooms (Selwyn 2014). Indeed, our research shows that such physical imagery of "the university" retains much of its symbolic strength in the context of distance and digital education (Bayne, Gallagher, and Lamb 2014). Yet digital education also enrolls misleading fantasies of education unbounded by material and temporal constraints, where students and teachers are infinitely nomadic, flexible, fluid, mobile. It often draws together the digital with notions of democratization and diversification, promising access to teaching, learning, and education regardless of where students are located or which time zone they inhabit. This fantasy of a weightless and untethered digital education can be contrasted with the monolithic physicality found in the prestigious steel and glass new university buildings and with the expensive renovation of iconic, historic buildings (Selwyn 2014). It can also obscure the other materialities that make such education possible: the physical infrastructures of connectivity involving cables, routers, mineral mining, server farms, toxic waste, and energy (Wajcman 2015); the precarious and casualized labor of teachers brought in to "deliver" it; and the brute inequality of access to the material and temporal resources still needed to attend college in any form (McMillan Cottom 2017).

While there are many researchers considering the various materialities of education infrastructure and politics, much educational theory and research on teaching practice continues to be focused on the sociality of learning. Material infrastructures are often rendered invisible or marginal, sidelined by a default assumption that the learning human subject is the only entity that really counts. Usher and Edwards (1994, 24) have critiqued this default humanism in the context of education for being based on

> an idea of a certain kind of subject who has the inherent potential to become self-motivated and self-directing, a rational subject capable of exercising individual agency. The task of education has therefore been understood as one of "bringing out," of helping to realise this potential, so that subjects become fully autonomous and capable of exercising their individual and intentional agency.

In this view, human agency is the supreme driver of the educational project, and the structural factors that constrain—or indeed enable—the exercise of that agency are rendered invisible. Education is seen as a process by which the individual moves toward being more fully human (Snaza 2014), making the human subject the center of educational processes and outcomes. This perspective views education as a process of socialization into prevailing cultural norms or as functioning to develop the "full potential" of an individual's capabilities. In either case, the core processes of education and learning are presented as fundamentally untroubled and unchanged by the material context in which they occur. In this context, technologies are often seen in terms of their capacity simply to assist and enhance human capabilities and so are understood as neutral instruments of human intention (Hamilton and Friesen 2013).

A growing body of research in education is working against these assumptions, bringing a posthumanist (or "more than human") sensibility to the study of teaching. This asks us to rethink our assumption that technology itself can be simply harnessed by teachers or students or unproblematically used to empower or drive better learning. Rather, we need to think of educational technology as produced through complex interactions between human and material entities within a specific, situated educational and political context. Technology changes teaching, and using technology well in the classroom means we have to rethink the definition of the classroom, and of teaching, itself.

Snapshot

In her 2009 book, *The Materiality of Learning,* Estrid Sørensen describes the challenges posed by the inclusion of a virtual world, Femtedit, in an educational assemblage. She emphasizes how the teacher in a physical classroom setting can monitor children within a bounded space, with full awareness of the key knowledge content of the textbooks used and the sequencing of learning activities. However, in the virtual world, children could interact with one another as avatars in unpredictable ways, and they could, and did, engage in continual processes of knowledge gathering and building by making and following hyperlinks within the virtual world. In this situation, the teacher was unable to know what knowledge content was being used or the sequencing of learning activities that were taking place.

The static objects of more conventional teaching practice such as textbooks and workbooks allowed the teacher to have a clear notion of what activities the students were, or should have been, engaged in. They created teaching as a controlled practice or even a practice of control. The tangle of dynamic sociality and materiality in the virtual environment, by contrast, produced unexpected and fluid patterns of activity in which hierarchical forms of control became impossible. To paraphrase Sørensen, the technologies of the virtual environment acted to challenge the traditional hierarchies of the classroom, placing the pupil and teacher at eye level.

We argue in our manifesto that digital education is best understood as a set of social and material practices involving complex interactions of humans and nonhuman entities. Material things and contexts are integral components of practice and co-constitute social action (Law 2004). Material objects are not passive instruments but active participants in the practices of education. Such sociomaterial approaches disturb established understandings of education "by making visible the everyday dynamics, particularly micro-dynamics of education and learning" (Fenwick and Landri 2012, 3–4). The material and the technological in this view are vital, active, generative, and autonomous: technologies produce their own effects. **The social is not the whole story.**

3

ONLINE TEACHING NEED NOT BE COMPLICIT WITH THE INSTRUMENTALIZATION OF EDUCATION.

Over recent decades, education has been reframed as a crucial component of economic health within the postindustrial context of the new capitalism, in which the primary sources of value are ideas, understanding, and intellect rather than physical and tangible assets (Sennett 2006; Moisio and Kangas 2016). Such a knowledge-based economy sees education primarily as a mechanism for enhancing human capital and an instrument of social and economic success. For example, a recent UK Government White Paper on Higher Education (BIS, 2016, 8–9) states:

> Graduates are central to our prosperity and success as a knowledge economy. . . . Research indicates that a 1% increase in the share of the workforce with a university degree raises long-run productivity by between 0.2% and 0.5%; and around 20% of UK economic growth between 1982 and 2005 came as a direct result of increased graduate skills accumulation.

The World Bank's Knowledge Assessment Methodology (World Bank Institute 2009, 1) identifies an educated population as a pillar of a knowledge economy in which people are required to "create and share knowledge, and to use it well." Similarly, the European Commission has linked education and economic competitiveness since its founding documents in the Treaty of Rome in 1957, and this continues in its education and economic strategies to the present day (Dima et al. 2018). In the United States also, education policy has been dominated by the priorities of skills development to sustain international economic competitiveness (Engel and Siczek 2018).

Public policy concerns with economic growth in this context are commonly translated and transformed into distinctly educational problems (Simons and Masschelein 2008, 395). Future economic growth is seen as being based on the ability of countries to generate employment opportunities in high-value occupations, with education framed as the way to achieve this. Such instrumentalization of education is reflected in the recommendations of supranational bodies such as the European Commission and Organization of Economic Cooperation and Development in their emphasis on collaborations of academics, business, and policymakers to generate and disseminate knowledge to meet the "needs of society."

A tension is created here between the framing of higher education as an instrument for promoting economic growth and its social and critical function, which seeks to understand and address the implications of that growth (Zgaga 2009). Within the instrumental view, higher education loses the wider political and critical role that is independent of government and corporations, risking becoming complicit in the reinforcement of existing political and economic injustices (Gewirtz and Cribb 2013, 80).

Munro (2018) argues that threaded through the discourses that position higher education as an instrument of national or regional economic competitiveness is a second discourse, which sees it as an instrument for personal financial advantage. This latter role is commonly articulated in terms of the employability of graduates and the so-called graduate premium—the additional earning power gained by achieving a university degree. It is also firmly embedded in tertiary and higher education policy imperatives. The European Union's Bologna process, for example, places employability at the center of higher education policy and purpose through the promotion of graduate attributes and a focus on the acquisition of in-demand skills and competencies (Sin, Tavares, and Amaral 2017). This supranational policy focus is also found in national policy discourses and institutional strategies (Gewirtz and Cribb 2013). In the United Kingdom, for example, the recent Augar Review of education after age eighteen and funding for England (Department for Education 2019) views the purposes of education in terms of national economic competitive advantage and personal financial benefit.

Recent UK government research found that the lifetime graduate premium for men was £168,000 and for women £252,000, compared to someone leaving education at age eighteen (Bolton and Hubble 2018). Internationally, the OECD (2018) found that the higher education systems in all member countries, with the exception of Austria, generated a graduate premium. The highest premiums were in Chile, at 264 percent, compared to 69 percent in the United States and 48 percent in the United Kingdom. Recent evidence from the United States, however, suggests a general flattening of the growth rate of the graduate premium (Ashworth and Ransom 2019).

Higher education institutions are thus understood as instruments of both national competitive advantage and individual aspiration, with knowledge being increasingly valued in instrumental terms (Selwyn 2014). Qualifications are seen as positional goods (Robertson and Olds 2018) that offer individuals a branded distinction in terms of future employability within higher-status occupations (Kretsos and Livanos 2016), while students themselves increasingly take a more instrumental approach to their studies, demanding greater perceived returns on their investment in education—the student as consumer (Walsh 2015).

The quest for qualifications here becomes an individual, and individualistic, response to the competitiveness and precariousness of modern working life (Tams and Arthur 2010). As John Warner (2018) argued on the Inside Higher Ed website, "Universities have come to understand themselves, at the highest levels, not as an investment for the public but as investment opportunities for one-percenters—with implications for everyone else." The decision to attend college is indeed now often framed in the language of cost-benefit analysis for the individual student (Browne 2010; Department for Education 2019).

We argue here that higher education is widely seen as an instrument of national and individual economic success—but why is the resistance to this idea particularly emphasized in the Manifesto for Teaching Online? Indeed, Jenny Mackness, commenting on an earlier version of this manifesto, has asked, "Does *any* teaching need to be complicit with the instrumentalisation of education?" (Mackness 2015, emphasis added). But digital education *is* often identified as something that is particularly friendly to the instrumentalization of education in both policy and individual terms, and we argue here that this takes place in two ways. First, that discourses of "the digital" are tightly entangled with those of the knowledge economy and employability, as part of a wider instrumental perspective on technology in general. Second, that digital education is often seen as aligned with the corporatization of higher education.

Digital education is commonly presented as part of a package of measures to more closely align higher education teaching with the needs or demands of a labor market by privileging digital competence (Conrads et al. 2017; Rivera-Velez and Thibault 2015). For example, King and Boyatt (2015, 1273) frame the adoption of digital education in terms of a perceived work readiness of students so they "leave higher education with the technological skills they will require in the workplace." Students are seen as expecting their higher education experiences to prepare them for digital work, and—in a context such as the United Kingdom, where only 50 percent of students believe their university experience has suitably prepared them for the digital workplace (Newman and Beetham 2017)—colleges oblige by requiring curricula and modes of teaching to include digital technologies. Digital education, especially as understood through the instrumental logic of "technology-enhanced learning" (Bayne 2015a), is enmeshed with notions of subordination to the knowledge economy.

The policy and popular discourses that align digital education with work readiness and employability in a digital economy present an example of the techno-instrumentalism that sees technology as a tool to be used for the realization of predefined political goals (Bayne 2015a; Hamilton and Friesen 2013). Technology is seen here as operating neutrally, "enabling the aims of educational endeavours but not influencing them" (Knox 2013b, 23), in this way echoing the instrumentalization of education itself as supporting the goal of national and individual economic success. Where technology is seen as merely a tool for delivering and enhancing education, it can only ever be valued for the extent to which it "works" or "enhances" a particular education practice or activity (Bayne 2015a; Knox 2013a). This sets digital education up perfectly as an instrument for the subordination of higher education to the demands of the knowledge-based society and the production of human capital.

Furthermore, digital education is also often understood as a gateway for the corporatization of higher education. Building infrastructure for digital education—for example, the implementation of learning management systems or lecture-recording technology—requires significant and visible monetary and other investments and so is generally dependent on top-down managerial change within universities (Singh and Hardaker 2017). As Noble (1998) pointed out in his early essay on "digital diploma mills," this centralization and standardization of teaching technologies undermines some long-held values in universities, such as the devolvement of decision-making, academic autonomy, and the ability for academics to be responsive, flexible teaching practitioners.

Digital education is often assumed to enable universities to generate surplus by delivering more education at less cost. Munro (2018) highlights how assumptions of cost efficiencies derived from investments in digital technologies are embedded in higher education policies in the United Kingdom through unproven assumptions of reduced teaching and assessment costs, reuse of learning materials and digital artifacts, and general economies of scale. Such assumptions can be found elsewhere, including Australia (Buchanan 2011) and North

America, where, Veletsianos and Moe (2017) argue, US federal policy discourses promote digital education on this basis.

Digital education is thus commonly entangled with the emergence of market-based rather than state-owned higher education (Veletsianos and Moe 2017) and commonly seen as a strong element of the disaggregation, or unbundling, that enables new for-profit providers to enter the sector (McMillan Cottom 2017; Williamson 2015). These may include specialist education service providers such as Pearson or Laureate, for-profit colleges such as the University of Phoenix, new platform entrants such as Udacity, and the megacorporations: Apple, Facebook, Google, and Microsoft (Walsh 2015). Digital technologies, and the promise they appear to offer for the efficient, profitable delivery of teaching at scale, have been readily aligned with the marketization of higher education and the reshaping of higher education to replicate the private sector.

However, we argue that digital education has a responsibility to be more explicit in its critical *non*complicity with such instrumental logics. Throughout this book, we aim to describe and map how we might do this through the practice of teaching. As just one example, Ross (2016) develops an approach that pushes back on techno-instrumental visions of maximal efficiency and profit by valuing the idea of a digital that welcomes uncertainty, risk, and complexity. Ross and Collier (2016) identify and celebrate the messiness involved in codeveloping online learning with students, nurturing multimodal and collaborative writing, working with the endless possibilities of the open Web, and other similar pedagogical possibilities that work best online. In the uncertainties of change and innovation can also be found the sources of hope for different and better education.

It is through such approaches that we can begin to engage in speculative explorations of alternative assemblages of digital education practice, building points of resistance to the dominant instrumental logics of how digital education *is* often used, and point toward ways in which it *might be* practiced otherwise. **Online teaching need not be complicit with the instrumentalization of education.**

4

ONLINE TEACHING SHOULD NOT BE DOWNGRADED TO "FACILITATION."

It has historically been common to emphasize the importance of online facilitation skills over the subject expertise or other, more specialist aspects of teacher professionalism when discussing digital education. The common perception in the early years of digital education that it was a fundamentally limiting mode of learning led commentators and practitioners to emphasize the importance of the effective facilitation of group sociality and learning in a context of reduced social cues (for a good example of this, see Feenberg and Xin 2010). While facilitation is of course an important aspect of teaching, we argue in this manifesto that good online teaching is very much more than this. We propose that an overfocus on the facilitation of learning has formed part of an arsenal of discourses that make digital education complicit with teacher deprofessionalization (Bayne 2015b; Selwyn 2014) and the commodification and instrumentalization of education itself (Munro 2018).

Digital practices are often seen as part of a wider tendency in education over recent decades to emphasize learning at the expense of teaching. This trend, famously labeled by

Biesta (2012) as "learnification," emphasizes the role of the autonomous learner over the professionalism of the teacher. It constructs education as an individualized and transactional process and minimizes discussion of the wider structural purposes and problems of education as a system and project.

The assumption that the individual student is an autonomous learner with a preexisting, fully developed sense of individual agency and purpose leads to a shift in the perceived role of the teacher, who in "learnified" discourses is often demoted from professional, expert provider to supporter and conduit for the self-determining individual learner. Learners are assumed to be competent to navigate the complexities of learning in ways that best suit their needs and can be best supported by making subject and discipline knowledge-objects available as efficiently as possible. As Biesta (2005) has pointed out, however, "a major reason for engaging in education is precisely to find out what it *is* that one actually needs—a process in which educational professionals play a crucial role because a major part of their expertise lies precisely there" (59). As we discussed previously, the practice of teaching cannot be reduced to the transmission of stable knowledge-objects alone.

In the context of digital education, and where learning is emphasized over teaching, it is often assumed that subject knowledge is most efficiently delivered by video lecture, podcast, or text resource, with course design being standardized and outsourced to instructional designers or other para-academic roles. The primary role of the teacher then becomes to lubricate, or facilitate, the social and dialogic aspects of learning in, for example, discussion forums, live chats, or video calls. The role of the teacher as subject matter expert and pedagogic architect is undermined.

The problem here is that such framings align tightly to reductive conceptualizations of education as a transactional process based on specified inputs generating predetermined outcomes for individual learners. Reducing the teacher function primarily to facilitation makes it easy to sideline the teacher as professional in the interests of efficiency, scalability, and individual consumer-learner choice. Movements in digital education that emphasize automation, scale and on-demand access often contribute to this deprofessionalization, making the delegation of the teacher function to automated systems or an underpaid, undervalued academic precariat seem supportable or even inevitable.

Digital technologies are often seen to enable the unbundling and devaluing of the teacher's role into discrete functional units such as subject matter expertise, instructional design, facilitation, learning support, pastoral care, assessment, and so on. In this way, much discussion of digital education seems to assume the desirability of the efficiency imperative: the standardization, routinization, and automation that undervalue subject expertise and the broader critical and social capabilities of the teacher, while overvaluing generic skills such as facilitation. Our own recent work has argued that learnification is intensified in new ways by digital and data technologies (Knox, Williamson, and Bayne 2019).

We argue in our manifesto that digital education is not inevitably complicit in the erosion of the teacher's role and professionalism. As we have suggested, teaching is situationally contingent and inherently multiple, with many "best" and "better" practices. Good education requires the exercise of teachers' professional and critical judgment in the context of the particular educational context in which they are working.

The increasing mobilization of digital technologies in the practices of education provides opportunities to rethink what both teaching and being a teacher mean. As it becomes clear that other actors beyond the human can be enrolled in the role of the teacher (Bayne 2015b; Dillenbourg 2016), so human teachers can engage in reflective learning on the effects of the digital in their professional practices (Littlejohn and Hood 2017). The professional judgment of teachers is central to how we understand the value of human and digital actors coming together to "do" and "do better" education.

High-quality education—as most teachers know—is inherently complex, subtle, and various, making the subjection of teaching to the procedural fantasies of standardization and routinization framed as best practice highly problematic. Digital education should not be complicit in replacing teaching—understood as a rich set of practices, often emergent with new technologies, but always highly professionalized—with reductionist notions of facilitation that place teacher subject expertise and critical professional judgment in the background of educational practice. **Online teaching should not be downgraded to "facilitation."**

5

CAN WE STOP TALKING ABOUT DIGITAL NATIVES?

Our manifesto makes the point—in different ways—that technology cannot be seen simply to determine how teaching will be done. Here we foreground one particularly damaging aspect of the deterministic language that has been regularly used to define students, the ways they learn, and the ways they should be taught. We argue that the highly problematic metaphor of the digital native is still too regularly used, continuing to negatively shape the way we understand the challenge of teaching online. Our argument is built around a critique of the essentializing nature of this term.

In defining what we mean by *essentializing*, we draw on the work of Hamilton and Friesen (2013) and their strong critique of digital education research from the perspective of science and technology studies. They describe digital education as being overly dependent on two simplistic, commonsense understandings of the nature of technology: the essentialist and the instrumentalist. Where instrumentalism sees technology as a neutral entity by which preexisting goals (for example, better learning) can be pursued, essentialism attributes to technology a set of "inalienable qualities" inextricably embedded within the technology itself (1). This kind of essentialism constructs a version of educational technology as separate from its social contexts, reducing the complex entanglements of the technological and social to a relationship of subordination: learning can be transformed by the built-in pedagogical value of certain technologies simply by allowing itself to be driven by them. Examples of this discourse common in contemporary ed-tech terminology include "unleashing the power of AI/data/IoT (etc.) to enhance learning" or "harnessing automation to scale education." The political implications of such calls to "innovate" are elided, as the technology is mythologized and essentialized.

Social scientists across many fields have shown how essentialist ideas play out in social contexts. For Kadianaki and Andreouli (2017), for example, the term refers to "ways of representing social categories as if they possessed an underlying essence, a fixed property, which determines the attributes of the members of these categories" (837). This essentialism of social categories is the frame by which we consider the metaphor of digital natives and immigrants here. To speak of digital natives is to use a reductive, essentializing category to describe entire generations. It is a metaphor that has been damagingly formative to the field of digital education, and it persists despite the large body of empirical research that has debunked it.

Posited most famously by Prensky (2001a) in a highly speculative commentary piece, the idea that there are essential differences between digital natives and digital immigrants, and in how different generations approach digital technologies, has remained influential in popular thinking about digital education and digital selfhood more generally. At any time, it is possible to search the news and find recent mobilizations of it, particularly in the business sector and in popular framings of governmental and supragovernmental policy. At the time of writing, the phrase had appeared in the preceding twenty-four hours in the UK *Daily Telegraph* (Turner 2018), an interview on the *Forbes* website (Munford 2018), and in a speech by European Union commissioner Mariya Gabriel (European Commission 2018).

In its reduction of complex social and technological change to a crude binary, the term continues to have a seductive appeal on first encounter, and an immediate resonance that predates Prensky's use of it. However, it is also deeply problematic in the way it marginalizes the professionalism of the teacher while normalizing a set of dangerously deterministic and colonialist metaphors. It proposes that young people have grown up in world where digital technology is ubiquitous, so they are naturally skilled with new digital technologies and spaces, while older people will always be a step behind and apart in their dealings with the digital. It further suggests that young learners' immersion in digital technologies prompts a new approach to learning, one that is concerned above all with dispositions aligned to the market rather than to conventional scholarship: speed of access, instant gratification, impatience with slowness, and dependence on the ability to multitask. Teachers in this context have often been described as having a duty to adapt their methods to this new way of learning, being required, in fact to reconstitute themselves according to the terms of the "native" in order to remain relevant and, presumably, employable.

Commentators and researchers have long considered the impact of new technology and media on young minds. Television drew negative attention for its impact on children and families in the 1970s (Winn 1977; Mander 1978) and more positive attention as "a primer on living in a discontinuous, cut-and-paste reality" in the 1990s (Rushkoff 1994, 124). By the late 1990s, digital culture was being subjected to similar kinds of commentary. In 1996 media analyst Douglas Rushkoff dubbed the children of the cyberage "screenagers" and compared them with the children of immigrants:

> Consider any family of immigrants to America. Who learns the language first? Who adopts the aesthetic, cultural, and spiritual values of their new host nation? The children, of course. . . . Well, welcome to the twenty-first century. We are all immigrants to a new territory. (Rushkoff 1996, 2)

A few years later, Prensky developed these ideas by adopting terminology used in the 1996 Declaration of the Independence of Cyberspace by Electronic Frontier Foundation founder John Perry Barlow, who had observed of his imagined audience, "You are terrified of your own children, since they are natives in a world where you will always be immigrants" (Barlow 1996). Prensky's two-part 2001 article, "Digital Natives, Digital Immigrants," consolidated Barlow's natives and immigrants metaphor in the public imagination and sparked a decade of academic debate and research. A large number of critiques appeared at the end of the 2000s (Helsper and Eynon 2010; Brown and Czerniewicz 2010; Jones et al. 2010; Selwyn 2009a; Hargittai 2010) questioning the evidence for the existence of digital natives in the (for the most part) university classroom. Bennett, Maton, and Kervin (2008), surveying the generational claims of Prensky and others, found a "clear mismatch between the confidence with which claims are made and the evidence for such claims" and saw "much of the current debate about digital natives [as] an academic form of moral panic" (782), one that unnecessarily established divides between different generations, between the technically adept and those who were not, between learners and teachers, and between "those who believe in the digital native phenomenon and those who question it" (782–783).

Prensky grounded his argument that young brains were being physically changed by new technologies in sketchily applied evidence from neurobiology and social psychology, emphasizing the brain plasticity that neuroscience has popularized in more recent years (Eagleman 2011; Ramachandran 2012). Clearly, immersing ourselves in a new information environment teaches us new skills and ways of thinking; if this were not the case, no form of education could teach us anything new. As we argue throughout this book, the social and the material are emergent with each other and indivisible. But this does not mean that the ability to learn through new media is a phenomenon embedded in the essence of what it means to be young.

The use of digital technologies and environments has become so much more widespread in the past two decades that we can see that spending large parts of our lives online changes us whatever our age. The flexibility that Prensky and others observed in the young in relation to new technology seems little more than an openness to explore it without prejudice. As digital technologies have become ubiquitous, we have all explored and adapted, and we continue to do so as the technology continues to change. Our manifesto's question about digital natives then is intentionally ambiguous and provocative. It is not only an inquiry (to which the answer, so far, is no), but a plea: Can we please stop talking about digital natives? To justify this, we consider here some fundamental critical objections to the term itself.

A central discomfort over the digital natives metaphor, and its flip side, the digital immigrant, relates to the notion of indigenousness or indigeneity: that is, that a native is indigenous to a specific place, or of that place, in a way that immigrants are not and cannot ever be. There are connections here with debates surrounding the relationship between settlers and indigenous peoples in postcolonial societies, labels that scholars argue are imprecise and complicated (Mamdani 2001; Davis 2017; Radcliffe 2017).

Mamdani (2001), one of "Africa's first generation of postcolonial intellectuals" (651), points out that in colonial Africa, "natives were said to belong to ethnic [cultural] groups; nonnatives . . . were identified racially [i.e., in biological terms, as white], not ethnically" (654). There are parallels here with the essentialism that describes all older people as digital immigrants, under an assumption that age, and therefore biology, trump personal experience, while younger people are imbued with a digital ethnicity by virtue of the technological culture that surrounds them. The digital natives/immigrants binary, however, inverts the colonial hierarchy, with digital skill, and thus power, seen to lie with the indigenous. Here, again, are parallels with Mamdani's portrait of postcolonial Africa, where "mainstream nationalists reproduced the dual legacy of colonialism. This time around, though, they hoped to privilege indigenous over nonindigenous citizens" (658).

Mamdani suggests that colonialism's crime was "to politicize indigeneity, first as a settler libel against the native, and then as a native self-assertion" (664). He seeks to prevent the proliferation of ethnically defined states and native authorities in postcolonial Africa by challenging the idea that we must define political identity, rights, and justice primarily in relation to indigeneity. As we have suggested, the category of digital native also fragments over time as waves of new technology shape successive generations of students differently. Challenging the dichotomy itself is surely, as for Mamdani, "the only way out" (663).

The complexities and sensitivities of the label of "native" in colonial and postcolonial societies prompt us to ask whether such concepts have any place in the digital realm. There are no first inhabitants from time immemorial of virtual spaces, only waves of newcomers over the past fifty or sixty years. Today's children are still born analogue. Many are, to different degrees, now raised digital, but the psychological and cultural differences this creates between them and their parents ought not be overstated. Digital skill and worldview are learned, not innate, and middle-aged immigrants of today have had far longer to learn them than their school-age children.

This less-used "digital immigrant" terminology has particularly unfortunate connotations at this current political moment, when immigration is being demonized by political populists throughout the world. Immigrants are cast in the popular imagination as never truly belonging to their adopted country, never being able to say that they are at home there—a charge that can become self-fulfilling. The immigrants of Prensky's dual metaphor may have receded somewhat into the background of popular commentary, but as long as the natives metaphor persists, then immigrants are present by implication.

In 2011 we explored the tensions inherent in this binary for teachers at a time when most were being cast as digital immigrants (Bayne and Ross 2011). We pointed out that by placing so-called digital natives in the "commanding position" and their immigrant teachers as "perpetually lacking and in need of development" (162), uncritical users of the terms effectively delegitimized and deprofessionalized teachers, and at the same time neutralized teachers' resistance to technology, however sound the reasons for that resistance might be. Any critique of technology, its role in education, or its implementation, we argued, as long as it comes from an "immigrant," can be quickly compartmentalized as belonging to a marginal, illegitimate voice.

We argued then, as now, that this discourse had—and still has—a paradox at its heart that is damaging for teachers. It normalizes a deeply essentializing vision of selfhood as determined by generational positioning, while also presenting an imperative for teachers and other professionals to constantly change and develop in order to remain relevant. It asks teachers to accept a position that is in permanent deficit and permanently precarious. Since the turn of this century and the emergence of the native/immigrant binary, we have seen this digital normalization of deficit and precarity become massively amplified with more recent waves of technological change. The global reworking of economies through the so-called fourth industrial revolution (Schwab 2016) and the promised upending of conventional understandings of professionalism by automation and datafication confront us with acute challenges as teachers, some of which we address in this book. Within such a context, it is surely time to move away from simplistic binaries to challenge essentializing and reductive ways of thinking about technological change, to look to diversity rather than dichotomy as we try to understand what it means to teach in a digital society. **Can we stop talking about digital natives?**

CONCLUSION: VALUING COMPLEXITY, VALUING THE TEACHER

Part I has provided an overview of some of the key ideas and arguments underpinning the Manifesto for Teaching Online, while addressing five particular statements:

There are many ways to get it right online. "Best practice" neglects context.

We should attend to the materialities of digital education. The social isn't the whole story.

Online teaching need not be complicit with the instrumentalization of education.

Online teaching should not be downgraded to "facilitation."

Can we stop talking about digital natives?

First, we used theories of sociomateriality and posthumanism to argue that teaching is a complex bringing together of people, text, images, sounds, locations, discourses, technologies, and modalities, by which we are able to open up practice to difference and critique. The highly situated, contextually contingent, and emergent properties of such gatherings enable multiple enactments of good teaching, not a homogenizing, normative goal of best practice. We argued instead for contextually sensitive teaching that seeks ways to acknowledge the materiality of the digital in digital education.

Then, by providing an overview of dominant contemporary digital education policies, trends, and trajectories, we argued that we can do better. By developing new conceptual and practice frameworks built around a critical sensibility that relishes complexity, we can move beyond the instrumental logics that have dominated digital education to date. Key to these practices will be a strong assertion of the value of the teacher and a focus on the importance of teachers' professional judgment and creativity, at a time when it risks being downgraded by the reductionist tendencies of contemporary ed-tech.

II

BEYOND WORDS

MANIFESTO POINTS COVERED

Text has been troubled: many modes matter in representing
academic knowledge.

Aesthetics matter: interface design shapes learning.

Remixing digital content redefines authorship.

Assessment is an act of interpretation, not just measurement.

A digital assignment can live on. It can be iterative, public,
risky, and multivoiced.

Figure 2.1

INTRODUCTION

In part II, we shift tack to talk about writing. We argue that conventional assumptions regarding authorship, originality, and assessment are challenged by digital learning and writing environments. Drawing on statements within the manifesto that cover themes of composition, communication, evaluation, and authorship, we argue that digital education requires us to rethink long-established understandings of originality, textual stability, and the representation of academic knowledge that are core to the way we have traditionally assessed and evaluated students' work. **Assessment is an act of interpretation, not just measurement.**

This places particular emphasis on how we understand authorship within a post-text context, creating particular challenges for teachers when it comes to assessing and evaluating student work. We do not mean this in the sense of dealing with plagiarism (discussed in part V) but rather in the more productive, positive sense of how we take account of the intellectual possibilities presented by shared authorship, collaboration, and digital remix when we grade student work. Digital authorship requires us to build a nuanced approach to design and interpretation, where the actions and interests of the student and teacher are bound to a wider network of human and nonhuman technologies and resources, opportunities and restrictions. **Remixing digital content redefines authorship.** Online assignments are not locked away in filing cabinets at the end of the academic year but can continue to circulate, grow, and be adapted, shared, and debated. **A digital assignment can live on. It can be iterative, public, risky, and multivoiced.**

Throughout chapters 6 to 10, we use the conceptual foundations of sociomateriality, explained in part I, to argue that meaning making is performed across a wide range of human and nonhuman agents and interests. The teacher, student, course work assignment, institution, technology, and a host of other interests are entwined in processes that mutually define one another and work inextricably toward the production of knowledge (Bayne and Ross 2013). This has potentially profound implications for how we understand authorial agency and the relation of this to the assessment and evaluation of academic work, individuation, and the methods we use for assessing—and awarding credit on the basis of—quality of knowledge representation.

Part II also draws on theories of multimodality in order to understand the changing nature of text and its place within scholarly work and teaching. The juxtaposition of botanical illustrations alongside written description in the earliest printed texts tells us that multimodal scholarship is far from a recent invention; however, its existence as a field of research is widely attributed to the work of Kress and Van Leeuwen

(2001). In particular, they called for greater attention to the ways that image, language, and other semiotic resources are woven together in the representation of meaning. Although multimodality accommodates a range of interpretations and applications, it tends to be supported by a small number of conceptual foundations we briefly describe (for a fuller overview, see Bezemer 2012).

This area of thought suggests that all representational acts are multimodal in the way that they are made up of a range of semiotic resources or modes, each with "special powers and effects" (Kress 2005), or potential to convey meaning. What we designate as a mode, including its powers of representation, is socially and culturally situated; as a result, there can be no universal taxonomy of modes. Similar to the way that sociomateriality recognizes that meaning is performed across a wide range of materials and bodies, multimodality demonstrates an openness to the full range of resources that have the potential to convey meaning, while taking a broad view of what might be assigned the status of a communicational or representational act. **Text has been troubled: many modes matter in representing academic knowledge.**

To put this into some educational context, a communicational act could be a lecture or lab report, a photograph or performance, and any other text where academic knowledge is conveyed. It can be an artifact, an instance of practice, or a combination of both. When a teacher uses presentation software in the classroom, a single slide might convey meaning through a juxtaposition of modes, including words, graphics, and sound effects. The color scheme and choice of font carry associations that shape how the audience interprets the material. As the teacher introduces the content on the slide, the multimodal text broadens to include the choice of language and the volume and tone of the spoken delivery, but also the teacher's posture, gesture, and gaze (Jewitt 2009). In these moments of preparation and performance, the teacher communicates through an orchestration of semiotic resources or modes in order to convey a particular meaning. Design, for Kress and Van Leeuwen (2001), "stands midway between content and expression" (5) and refers to the deployment of modes to communicate meaning in a given situation. **Aesthetics matter: interface design shapes learning.** As will become apparent as the chapters in this part unfold, in the context of digital education, this deployment works in different ways across multiple kinds of digital artifacts and practices.

6

TEXT HAS BEEN TROUBLED: MANY MODES MATTER IN REPRESENTING ACADEMIC KNOWLEDGE.

In the context of the manifesto, *text* can be read in two ways. First, it refers to the printed word, the dominant means of representing academic knowledge since the fifteenth-century invention of the Gutenberg press (Ong 1960). In this sense, it can equally refer to the meticulously typeset words of a monograph, the rapidly assembled smartphone message, or a paragraph copied from one screen-mediated document and then pasted into another. From a multimodal perspective, however, *text* has tended to be used in a broader way to denote a representational genre: written or printed text but also painting, photograph, poetry recital, music performance, and so on. Genre, according to Bateman (2008), provides a way of framing discussion around multimodality and of theorizing what a multimodal document can be. As multimodality has emerged as a discrete field of research alongside and often closely tied to advances in digital technology (Kress and Selander 2012), a considerable amount of its interest has concerned the construction and interpretation of different genres of digital texts.

A central proposition of multimodal research is that the proliferation of digital devices and platforms across education and society has made it increasingly easy to communicate across a range of semiotic resources—that is, materials and actions that carry meaning.

Combining both interpretations of text, the Manifesto for Teaching Online argues that digital education—and digital society generally—offers us new ways of communicating and consuming academic knowledge. The essay, textbook, and journal article, whether presented on paper or screen, remain central, yet the repertoire of resources we can plausibly use to share scholarship has broadened. Within digital learning environments, teachers and students can readily draw on the representational possibilities of games, visualizations, videos, podcasts, animations, illustrations, and more (Bayne and Ross 2013; Bezemer and Kress 2008; McKenna and Hughes 2013). This is not to suggest that academic knowledge has previously been limited to the power of words: anatomical drawings, architectural models, data visualizations, and a multitude of artifacts and practices within the creative arts illustrate a deep-rooted tradition of multimodal meaning-making across the disciplines. At the same time, while assignments constructed in digital form support diverse media that cannot be deployed in conventional printed forms, these new media spaces can just as easily replicate the linearity, structure, and other conventions of the word-processed essay (McKenna and McAvinia 2011). Nevertheless, across a range of academic contexts (and particularly in settings that have traditionally privileged written text) the digital form presents new opportunities for constructing and sharing academic knowledge in ways beyond words.

The case for placing greater emphasis on multimodality within teaching has been made in a number of ways across the literature, including the need for pedagogy to take advantage of emergent digital technologies (Matthewman and Triggs 2004) and to acknowledge the evolving literacy practices of students (Krause 2013). Multimodal pedagogy is also seen to align with our increasingly visual society (Bickmore and Christiansen 2010) and better equip learners with the meaning-making practices demanded by employment (Kimber and Wyatt-Smith 2010) and the global economy (Johnson and Kress 2003). However, rather than looking to the way that digital multimodal education can deterministically align to the pressures of the knowledge economy critiqued in part I of this book, in this manifesto statement, we are interested in how a multimodal slant within teaching can play a critical role, offering new, highly creative ways for students to represent what they know for the purposes of assessment, sharing, and evaluation. Allowing, or even requiring, students to look to genres and modes beyond text prompts them to think both critically and creatively about what it means to represent academic knowledge.

Within our master's in digital education program, we use this approach to ask students to challenge and question some of the orthodoxies of linearity, authorship, and mode while also offering them a wide digital palette with which they can experiment with radically divergent ways of building an academic argument. We ask them to address the implications of the visual turn in the wider culture for academic ways of knowing by experimenting with technologies that place a greater emphasis on visuality (Carpenter 2014; McKenna and McAvinia 2011), exploring digital alternatives to the dominance of language-as-text in its different forms. This does not mean that the image will necessarily entirely displace words on page or screen but instead that, as teachers, we can be open to alternative and other representational possibilities. Taking the position that all communicational acts are multimodal to some degree, our manifesto statement should be seen not as a call to exclude printed text, but rather to better acknowledge and accommodate the representation of academic knowledge in ways beyond words.

Snapshot

One of our students, J. D. Caudle, produced a multimodal essay for his final course assessment in which he explored, among other things, how affect and emotion can be wrought in new ways through digital text and what this might mean for academic writing. As part of this, he created within his digital essay a section of text that functioned as a "minefield': when the cursor is run over the text, it causes at certain random points an explosion with image and sound effects that are (mildly) shocking to the reader. He rationalizes his design choice in terms of how digital sensory experience can force affect in a way that is impossible in conventional printed text:

By creating a "minefield" of invisible cursor-sensitive regions of a digital text, image, or other space, the [reader] is forced to engage with the content in a context of uncertainty and danger. Unexpected and violent sensory experiences are triggered by the "mines." This combination of uncertainty and violence could create emotional associations with the text. Invisible boundaries are enacted for the [reader], with some degree of approximation; there are obviously dangerous and safe areas, but the boundaries between those are not precisely defined. (Caudle 2016)

Other students have embedded self-designed games in essays on game-based learning; developed essays entirely in game form; recorded Google Streetview flyovers to describe mobile learning; created open educational resources to offer their ideas for global reuse; overlaid their scholarship onto video and poetry; created image composites, written songs, and written code; and created rabbit holes of interlinked digital text. In assessing and assigning grades for such work, we always look to the quality of the academic argument extended. This is not just about digital play for its own sake, but about how digital and other media can extend the critical force of an argument.

Perhaps understandably in light of its historical commitment to the printed word, much of the critical discussion around multimodality and pedagogy in the literature is set within the humanities and disciplines, which have tended to privilege written language. In particular, there has been an interest in assessment approaches that offer greater representational flexibility than is possible with the traditional essay—for instance, through the creation of animations (Gunsberg 2015), video games (Colby 2014), and visually oriented artifacts such as posters (Archer 2011). Compared to the essay genre with its deep-rooted textual orthodoxies of linearity, structure, and form, the digital environment offers students greater scope to experiment with alternative ways of building an academic argument. It also, of course, carries potential disadvantages: the removal of well-established constraints such as tightness of word count, elegance of exposition, and use of existing literature brings with them a loss of established frameworks for assessing quality, making multimodal assignments often harder to assess and grade.

The possibility exists that teachers might be more enthusiastic about embracing multimodality than students, who may be reluctant to experiment with the "dubious" and "disposable" digital form (Bayne 2006, 21), particularly in the high-stakes assessment setting where the tried-and-trusted essay approach might seem considerably less risky (Lea and Jones 2011). As discussed in part I, we should also remain alert to the way that educational activity is assembled by many agents (Fenwick, Edwards, and Sawchuk 2011), including the teacher and student but extending beyond. Therefore, where research around multimodal pedagogy usefully highlights some of the representational and interpretive challenges that exist around the creation of academic content, sociomateriality enables us to better understand how a piece of digital scholarship can be shaped by learning outcomes and the learner's interests, but also through the availability and capability of technologies, institutional decisions around procurement and benchmarking, as well as by resources of time, money, and support.

We argue that with some groups of students, allowing the wide, creative scope of the multimodal, digital assignment produces work of high quality and high value. To take such an approach requires us as teachers to develop—for ourselves and for our students—new ways of approaching the task of assessment and evaluation that move us beyond the long-established textual orthodoxies and into challenging new territory. **Text has been troubled: many modes matter in representing academic knowledge.**

7

AESTHETICS MATTER: INTERFACE DESIGN SHAPES LEARNING.

Just as the orchestration of resources within a digital artifact will influence representations of academic knowledge, design decisions concerning the platforms and networked spaces where teaching takes place have an impact on pedagogy. From a technical perspective, the term *interface* is broadly understood to denote an application or program that enables a user to communicate with a computer or a comparable digital device. From an online teaching perspective, the most obvious example of an interface might be the institutional learning management system (LMS), where a student can access essential course information, including assessment details, timetables, lecture slides, and reading lists. In the higher education setting, it has also become the place where students submit assignments. The LMS is normally accessed using a university portal and often links to academic databases, discussion boards, and other networked environments. Therefore, the LMS is an interface itself, but it also acts as a gateway to a series of other interfaces over which the teacher and institution have varying degrees of control.

In the overtly multimodal and visually rich spaces of the Web, the challenge of building an online course presence includes individual teachers in thinking about accessibility, content, and navigation, but also how layout, color, font, image, and other design devices support and enhance opportunities for learning. Individual teachers rarely have meaningful control over the design of the institutional LMS interface they use. Yet even here, and in the absence of any design background or training, when the teacher scrolls down the list of possible typefaces or drags the cursor across the palette of background colors, he or she will be guided by a tacit understanding that the choice made will influence the interpretation of the meaning that is conveyed. Arial is almost certainly better than Papyrus in setting the tone for a course on political activism, for instance. In this way, the design choices teachers make can subtly influence learning through the way that students are guided toward a particular conceptualization of the course and its pedagogy.

The relationship between interface design and learning can also be usefully explored through the example of the discussion forum that has become synonymous with online teaching. At the point of creating the discussion forum, the teacher exercises some degree of control over the structure, function, and appearance of the discussion forum. This might include aesthetic choices concerning template and layout, perhaps followed by assigning administrative privileges, establishing who will be entitled to open new threads of discussion, and whether conversation will be presented in cascading style. Design decisions taken at the point of configuring the forum can have considerable bearing on whether students choose to follow and contribute to conversation or whether discussion moves to another networked space (or simply falls silent). The choices described here can influence whether the individual student chooses to share his or her ideas with the class, but can also more broadly help to negotiate a particular course ambience and ethos. Going further, as the teacher establishes rules relating to member status, posting privilege, and approval, he or she can engender (or challenge) particular course power relations while projecting a presence that manifests beyond class discussion. Meanwhile, informality and collaboration might be nurtured by arranging activities in social media spaces, or what Fitzpatrick (2011a) refers to as the "profoundly dialogic spaces of the web."

As teachers monitor the discussion forum or uploads a list of resources to the course site, their status in the function tab of the LMS might be suggestive of the multiple roles they have come to perform: author, administrator, student mode. If these different editing designations imply an ownership or control over the representational and functional elements of the learning platform, from a sociomaterial perspective, the teacher-designer agency is situated within a wider assemblage of opportunities, interests, pressures, and resources. The educational interface is a complex assemblage of visible and invisible materialities beyond the immediate control of the teacher. While some teachers will have reasonable freedom to make decisions around the selection and configuration of different learning environments, many others will be tied in to the systems and spaces that are supported by the institution. Inevitably, institutional strategy and procurement decisions are unlikely to meet the pedagogical needs of every course of study or cohort of learners.

When each interface brings its own possibilities and constraints that shape its perception and use by students, the newly acquired LMS might be welcomed by the teacher who likes to communicate a body of knowledge through video lectures, but could prove inadequate for a colleague whose teaching depends on synchronous discussion and interaction. Going further, a sociomaterial attention to the wider network of materialities of educational practice also draws our focus to the influence of code buried within the interface of the application (Edwards and Carmichael 2012). As Selwyn (2009b) argues in his discussion of the connectivities of digital education, the code that exists beneath learning platforms can shape social relations and structure in hierarchy in ways that are counter to the pedagogic aims of the course itself. Therefore, where aesthetically informed decisions around interface design can influence the nature of online learning, we are reminded that teachers do not exercise sole agency even when they have reasonable freedom to choose the platforms where learning will take place. When a teacher glances at her designated editing status at the corner of the wiki or course web page, she might consider that her authorial agency is shared with a multitude of other social and material interests beyond the academic content she wants to share with students.

Our manifesto point draws attention to this complexity and its implications for teachers. We emphasize what we see as a neglected aspect of higher education pedagogy generally, but particularly in its digital forms: its aesthetic and design dimensions and the power relations that flow from these. We are, rightly, asked to be well versed in how to ensure accessibility of digital teaching resources to all students regardless of their specific learning needs; however, we are rarely asked to reflect on the everyday design decisions we make as we carve learning spaces out of institutional LMSs for ourselves and our students. LMSs themselves are generally not particularly friendly to the idea of teacher flexibility and control of interface, to the extent that building an online course is often seen as being the responsibility of learning technologists or other learning support professionals. Yet this kind of unbundling of the teaching role may well not be appropriate where there are complex, responsive, and subtle decisions to be made about the structural organization of our digital classrooms and the social relations that cascade from these. As teachers, we need to be able to assert the pedagogic aesthetic that is right for our students. **Aesthetics matter: interface design shapes learning.**

8

REMIXING DIGITAL CONTENT REDEFINES AUTHORSHIP.

A considerable amount of what we understand about the nature of scholarship, including authorship practice, is disrupted within digital environments. Within this manifesto statement, we consider the academic author to be the scholar expounding on her area of expertise in a monograph, but also the recently enrolled undergraduate who is uncertainly composing his first course work assignment. Although the level of expertise and experience might differ, the professor and student are united by the idea of the author as an individual in possession of a creative agency through which the text is crafted and stabilized. Authorship has tended to be seen as the practice of individually or jointly producing the research paper, lab report, or other artifact of scholarship. The nature of authorship becomes more complex, however, within increasingly digital compositional environments. Bayne (2006) draws on Foucault's (1977) poststructuralist conception of the author function and Poster's (2001) ideas around analogue and digital authorship to argue that authorship is troubled by digital environments, while Fitzpatrick (2011b) recognizes the representational possibilities of the remix or mash-up where the creator's words are woven together with visual, aural, and other web-based content. The ease with which we can browse, download, and then reuse networked material provides new ways of representing academic knowledge while also altering the nature of authorship itself. For Fitzpatrick (2011b), we

> find our values shifting away from a sole focus on the production of unique, original new arguments and texts to consider instead curation as a valid form of scholarly activity, in which the work of authorship lies in the imaginative bringing together of multiple threads of discourse that originate elsewhere, a potentially energizing form of argument via juxtaposition. (11–12)

In using the term *juxtaposition* here, Fitzpatrick draws our attention to the orchestration of scholarship that can take place when we write online. For example, a scholar might intersperse his own written commentary with YouTube clips or embed direct, click-through links to the writing of others, or weave in images and audio pulled from multiple external sources. This provides particularly rich compositional possibilities for the student authors as they are able to draw on different voices while simultaneously working across genres, bringing together the representational powers of pictures, sounds, and words. One consequence of this digitally mediated and multimodal rich scholarship, however, is the question it provokes around attribution and citation. To put it more simply, when a student embeds a film clip, imports a stock photo, or downloads a soundtrack to help advance his or her ideas, the teacher might ask whether this compromises the student's claim to authorship, with implications for assessment that we discuss in chapter 9. Or, conversely, the teacher might see a student's ability to source and then configure digital material as a kind of curatorship and argumentation that should be recognized and rewarded.

The evolving character of authorship in digital environments also, according to Adami (2012), has implications for power as well as the nature of composition. A cut-and-paste culture supports new opportunities for the production of multimodal texts but also, in Adami's view, facilitates the reproduction of networked content out of context, thereby raising questions about authorial responsibility and power. Of course, there is nothing new in a student misjudging how a quote or other piece of supporting evidence might translate from journal article to essay; the significance, however, lies in the ease with which a rapidly deployed key command can replicate chunks of content from the ostensibly social space of the Web within a piece of scholarship. In this way, the conventional assignment can resemble less an essay than a collage or commonplace book. Therefore, the reuse of networked content that characterizes the mash-up or remix assignment certainly presents new possibilities for the representation of academic knowledge, but at the same time provokes important and complex questions for teachers about authorship, quality, and authenticity. Going further, the position that an educator or institution adopts in relation to the nature of authorship in increasingly digital and multimodal contexts needs to reflected in pedagogy, for instance, within learning outcomes and the dialogue with students that takes place around assessment (Lamb 2018). If nothing else, as long as we are going to allow, encourage, or require students to demonstrate ability and understanding in images and audio, we should spend time exploring with them issues around copyright and attribution in the same way that attention is currently given to discouraging plagiarism in written material.

If remix scholarship sits uneasily with some of the deeply rooted assumptions about originality within education, authorship is redefined in a much subtler way through the working of code within the devices, software, and search engines drawn into the creation of academic digital artifacts. Considered from a sociomaterial perspective, the computer-aided drawing, blog post, and multimedia essay cannot be solely attributed to the individuated human author but instead can be seen as emerging from a multitude of human and material interests. These agents include the algorithmic operations that structure and shape the interface by which the article or assignment is prepared. For example, the intrusion of personalized advertisements in a student blog post, targeted according to the browser history and data trail of the teacher reading it, is authored by the environment and shaped according to the commercial interests of the blog platform rather than by the student, but nonetheless becomes part of the submitted blog post.

While technology has always been implicated in the production of academic knowledge, there is a considerable difference between the content-generating possibilities of contemporary hardware and software and the previous technologies of rollerball pen and refill pad, for example. The typical smartphone presents the opportunity to record, edit, and share a short film to a standard that until relatively recently would have been limited to those with considerable technical expertise and access to expensive equipment. The same device, used to download special effects and browse how-to videos, promises shortcuts for the student who has never attended a film production class or visited an editing studio. Therefore, when digital technology is heavily implicated in the creation of the digital artifact, code becomes a coauthor within a complex assemblage of interests extents far beyond the student submitting the assignment or, as Gourlay and Oliver suggest (2013): "Authorship becomes distributed, interwoven between machine and human, as opposed to being associated with a singular, embodied human subject. In this conception, texts are produced by multiple, hybrid biological entities meshed with wide online networks through the writing process" (82).

To ask a student to create work within such a context requires an openness on the part of the teacher—and the institution within which both are embedded—to these new forms of authorship. When stability and authenticity of a text owned by a single student author gives way to juxtaposition, remix, and sharing, conventional methods of establishing the quality of student work are placed under significant pressure. If we want to adopt such methods—and we argue that we should want to, where it is appropriate—we need to be able to develop new standards and norms for how we measure the standard of student work. **Remixing digital content redefines authorship.**

Snapshot

Prompted by an interest in the way that the academic remix disrupts conventional ideas of authorship, in 2016 members of our digital education team established an online project, Composition: Conversation about Content and Form. With an emphasis on combining creativity and criticality, students and other scholars are encouraged to produce and submit richly multimodal artifacts that respond to excerpts or ideas from conventional print-mediated journal articles and book chapters. To date, this has included a collage of field recordings, captions, and moving images that explored Silva and Frith's (2010) work around location and spatial identity and a visual creation that drew on classic science-fiction themes to explore cyborg culture in the writing of Miller (2011), Haraway (1991), and Richardson (2007). After publishing the work on the project website alongside a short written rationale, commentators from a range of disciplines are invited to comment on the remix, with their responses being shared beneath the work. The combined effect of the original piece of scholarship, its reinterpretation, and then the reaction it provokes is to produce a multilayered piece of composition that challenges the conventional stability and ownership we tend to associate with academic content. The original language-based exposition of meaning extends to include the representational possibilities of image and sound, while the single author's voice is transformed into an interdisciplinary conversation that plays out across the Web rather than within the pages of a stable academic text (http://newcomposition.weebly.com/).

9

ASSESSMENT IS AN ACT OF INTERPRETATION, NOT JUST MEASUREMENT.

The changing nature of authorship described in this part, combined with the increasingly multimodal character of meaning-making, carries implications for teachers when they are called to evaluate the quality of an assignment presented in digital form. The need for interpretive judgment is not a product of online teaching; on the contrary, assessment instruments across all disciplines call on teachers to interpret meaning as they examine and grade student work, despite grading being commonly understood as the measurement of student learning. Through this manifesto statement, however, we argue that the digital assignment foregrounds this interpretive dimension, creating a need for new, responsive ways of understanding and providing feedback on such work. We have already argued that multimodal representation provokes new possibilities and questions around scholarly composition and authority; it also brings challenges at the point of assessment. It is reasonable to assume that teachers who served their academic apprenticeship in the predominantly text-oriented humanities might not feel they have the repertoire of interpretive skills to measure the quality of an assignment where argumentation is presented through an orchestration of language, image, sound, or any other modes and media. How do the conventions of the neatly crafted written argument translate to streamed music or a moving image? One approach to this interpretive challenge, we argue, involves holistically considering the combined effects of all the different resources within an assignment rather than attempting to examine the merit of each mode in isolation. This approach aligns with one of the cornerstones of multimodality, where the meaning depends on the combined effects of the full range of resources within a representational act.

There also exists the interpretive challenge of establishing how much of the overall impact of the argument of the assignment relies on the student's ideas and decisions compared with the built-in possibilities of the software or platform where it was constructed. To put it another way, how is the teacher to locate the student's imagination, technical ability, or critical capacities within a web essay, animation, or presentation submitted for assessment? There might be a case for rewriting assessment criteria and learning outcomes in order to recognize the design decisions that are part of the compositional process (see, for example, Shin and Cimasko 2008), as well as engaging in ongoing discussion with students about the purpose and expectations of the multimodal assignment (Bourelle, Bourelle, and Jones 2015). Or in the absence of ongoing dialogue with the student around her compositional intentions, the teacher might ask that with the submitted assignment, the student provide a rationale (Coleman 2012) or reflective documentation (Colby 2014) that sets out the creative process or learning that has taken place behind the work.

Snapshot

Our approach to the assessment of digital assignments is to grade partly on the basis of criteria that the students themselves set. We use preset criteria covering knowledge and understanding of concepts, knowledge and use of the literature, and constructing academic discourse but invite students to identify up to three of their own criteria in addition to these that are appropriate to the particular media and modes chosen. Some examples of student-nominated criteria include "production of a deliverable that other members of the community can benefit from and build upon," "the relationship between technology and content—does method of delivery aid the effectiveness of the argument?" "visually interesting," and "it should make you smile at least once." This final criterion prompted us to remember that at times, we need to refind the pleasures of reading and grading student work. As Fitzpatrick (2011b) has framed it:

We all need to rethink our authorship practices, not only because the new digital technologies becoming dominant within the academy are rapidly facilitating new ways of working and new ways of imagining ourselves as we work, but also because such reconsidered writing practices might help many of us find more pleasure in the act of writing itself. (3)

A similar interpretive challenge can exist around the assessment of the remix assignment we described. In these instances, the teacher might need to establish the extent to which the work depends on an externally authored video and soundtrack compared with the input of the student whose name appears in the opening titles or across the front page. The interpretive act in this situation might involve establishing the prominence of the student's authorial voice compared with his or her ability to source and curate networked content. Considerably more complex, however, is the question of whether authorship extends to the algorithm and code beneath the interface of the compositional software and search engines that may have helped the assignment to take shape. If we accept that all educational activity is performed through an assemblage of the social and material (Fenwick, Edwards, and. Sawchuk 2011), then this would also seem to apply to assignments presented for submission. As teachers cast an eye over the reference list at the end of the web essay (or perhaps within the rolling credits of a video assignment), they might reflect on whether, in light of institutional regulations about plagiarism and academic misconduct, the student has an obligation to acknowledge the range of individuals without whom it would not have been possible to realize the assignment in digital form. Considered from a sociomaterial stance, the teacher might ask where, among the names associated with book chapters and journal articles, is an acknowledgment of the designers, coders, focus group participants, fundraisers, and factory workers whose industry and inspiration are entangled in the Web essay that bears a single student's name.

The relationship between algorithms and education is considered in more length in chapter 13: **Algorithms and analytics recode education: pay attention!** We also look at the question of plagiarism in more depth in part V. Our interest at this point has simply been to draw attention to the range of interpretive challenges that exist around assessment in digital contexts. If the individuation of the student author becomes problematic in the context of the digital assignment, we must ask some fundamental questions about the nature of assessment itself and, by extension, the credentialing on which much of the value of formal education is based. **Assessment is an act of interpretation, not just measurement**.

10

A DIGITAL ASSIGNMENT CAN LIVE ON. IT CAN BE ITERATIVE, PUBLIC, RISKY, AND MULTIVOICED.

Beyond the issues around establishing authorship and interpreting quality, teachers also have to reckon with the public and temporal nature of assessment in digital environments. Summative assessment is generally seen as a more-or-less private exchange between student and teacher, and it is generally the case that the student relinquishes authorial power over the assignment at the point that it is submitted. Other than in special circumstances, the evolution of the assignment halts at the point of submission. Digital assignments, however, carry within them the possibility of extending and growing beyond this point of submission and beyond this private relationship. There is an overflow of the moment in time within which the conventional written essay is submitted and fixed.

A feature of the increasingly digital nature of society and teaching is the possibility of presenting scholarship across networked platforms, including those in the public domain. The student who builds an digital assignment beyond the networked space of the institution—for instance, using a blog, a repository, or social media environment— is able to exercise continuing editorial control that is normally conceded when the conventional essay is uploaded to the submission box of the institutional LMS or deposited on the teacher's desk. Where the traditional assignment lies dormant awaiting the teacher's attention, the digital assignment lives on. The grader may have taken receipt of a link to the online assignment; however, the student at least notionally retains the ability to continue revising it. This is suggestive of a new dynamic of power relations when a digital assignment is hosted beyond the institution's space. The teacher's ability to enforce a deadline or achieve equity across the class is problematic when some assignments continue to evolve, perhaps even beyond the point that they have been graded and assigned feedback. If the student chooses to promptly revise the assignment in line with the grader's comments, the work considered by the external examiner at the end of the semester—as is normal in the United Kingdom and certain other national contexts—might be considerably different from what was previously reviewed.

The sustained life of the digital assignment enables students, should they wish, to reuse their work or open it to a global public to enable others to learn from it. Of course, this also carries risk for the student author. If some learners might welcome the ability to improve a piece of work in perpetuity, for others it could represent a kind of tyranny as they continually strive for an idealized state of perfect completion. The temptation to tinker is likely to be even greater when work is hosted in a public networked space and potentially subject to scrutiny from a wider audience, whether real or imagined. For the student mapping a particular career trajectory, the networked assignment might become part of an extended online curriculum vitae, something to be publicized (or, conversely, concealed from view through acts of networked curation). The lasting presence of the online assignment raises the prospect that a student might be discouraged from experimenting or confronting contentious subject matter when his or her work could potentially be viewed and commented on outside the context in which it was created.

As well as ceding control over who views her work, the student might also find that the assignment continues to evolve without her input or approval. Within our own teaching, students have sometimes built course work assignments within *Minecraft* and, previously, in the *Second Life* virtual world. The public and collaborative nature of these spaces means that the work sometimes remains active as it is adapted or occupied by individuals or avatars with no connection to the original creation. Elsewhere, the life of the animation, short film, or live performance hosted on a video channel is sustained as visitors post comments or hit the Like button below the original work. The pages of Vimeo and YouTube offer countless first drafts and final assignments that continue to receive feedback long after the creator will have graduated from high school or college. In the case of audio assignments uploaded to an interactive space like SoundCloud, listeners are able to assign feedback to specific parts of the track, thereby providing a kind of critical commentary alongside the original recording. As discussion unfolds alongside or beneath the original podcast or video, the exposition of meaning is altered and the assignment becomes multivoiced as the viewer's attention flickers between the assignment and the reaction it has generated. **A digital assignment can live on. It can be iterative, public, risky, and multivoiced**, for better or worse.

Snapshot

The dynamism and longevity of the digital assignment particularly come to the fore when produced within the context of an open online course. Our manifesto offers a view on the openness of open education explained in part III of this book; however, it is sufficient for the moment to note the open movement's interest in the production and performance of educational materials and practices that exist beyond the publisher's paywall or the log-in of the university LMS. In a keynote delivered at the seventh Open Educational Resources Conference, Jim Groom (2016) discussed the digital storytelling course he created at the University of Mary Washington. The course encourages a creative and collaborative approach where students consume and construct a range of digitally mediated work across the open spaces of the Web. During his keynote, Groom described how participant-generated work such as the blogpost, infographic, and poster were able to quickly reach a wide audience on account of being published to the Web. If this talks to us about the possibilities of rapidly distributing academic content across networked spaces, there is an equally interesting story to be told around the extended life and evolving character of these different digital assignments and artifacts. In contrast to work that is laid to rest in the departmental office or the drop box of a learning management system, the online presence of these digital assignments enabled them to live on as they provoked below-the-line comments and were placed in juxtaposition with other digital content.

CONCLUSION: BEYOND WORDS, BEYOND THE AUTHOR

In this part, we have worked across themes of composition, knowledge representation, authorship, and assessment to argue that some deeply rooted assumptions about teaching are unsettled as it increasingly takes place in digital environments. In particular, we have expanded the following manifesto statements:

Text has been troubled: many modes matter in representing academic knowledge

Aesthetics matter: interface design shapes learning

Remixing digital content redefines authorship

Assessment is an act of interpretation, not just measurement

A digital assignment can live on. It can be iterative, public, risky, and multivoiced

When education is shaped by complex software and the collaborative spaces of the internet, we have argued that we can no longer default to the notion of the individuated, autonomous human author but need to take account of new, volatile patterns of composition and sharing. As we have shown, this has potentially profound implications for the creation and conceptualization of work that students submit for assessment and, in turn, how teachers assess, grade, and comment on assignments.

Drawing on ideas from the literature on multimodality, we have highlighted some of the key representational possibilities and interpretive challenges that are provoked when scholarship is presented in digital form. The composition of a digital artifact is not attributable solely to the individual student; it instead emerges from a complex entanglement of social and material agents concerned with technology, pedagogy, institutional strategy, and beyond. As teachers, digital education challenges us to think in a new way about the nature of assessment and the practices of grading, including what it means to construct meaning in multimodal and technologically rich contexts. We need to ask who, and what, is responsible for the scholarly work that is presented across the screen and think again about the value claims we can make when we assign grades and credit through assessment practices forged and normalized in an earlier media age.

III

RECODING EDUCATION

MANIFESTO POINTS COVERED

Openness is neither neutral nor natural: it creates and depends
on closures.

Massiveness is more than learning at scale: it also brings complexity and diversity.

Algorithms and analytics recode education: pay attention!

Automation need not impoverish education: we welcome our
new robot colleagues.

Figure 3.1

INTRODUCTION

Part III connects, by way of critical analysis, four points made within the Manifesto for Teaching Online and four phenomena currently prominent within digital education: the open education movement, massive open online courses (MOOCs), algorithmic functions in education technology, and automation. These areas have received much attention in recent years, and here we provide background to the manifesto points that challenge some of the dominant assumptions that surround them. Both open education and data-driven technologies have promised significant disruptions, proposing visions of egalitarian access to educational opportunities and new kinds of scientific precision in how we "do" teaching. While these ideals have merit, it is important to look beyond the hyperbole and attempt to understand the broader political, social, and economic contexts in which they are situated.

First, open education is examined through two examples that provide the means to examine how openness is portrayed in education: the Year of Open proposed in 2017 by the Open Education Consortium, and the OER World Map project funded by the Hewlett Foundation. The chapters in this part focuses on interrogating the assumptions of neutrality and inherent value that too often accompany the discourse of open education and offers a number of critical perspectives through which scholarship and practice in this area might be developed. We argue in chapter 11 that **Openness is neither neutral nor natural: it creates and depends on closures.**

Second, this part examines the recent proliferation of open courses, often aligned or associated with scale and the MOOC. The enrollment numbers in these courses, routinely emphasized in media hyperbole at the time when they emerged (around 2012–2013) aligns, we argue, with a negative framing of openness that assumes a narrow definition of educational access. The attempt to globalize education through such courses, we suggest, enacts a problematic kind of standardization and promotes a corporate vision of the rational, self-directing learners we discussed in part I and which continues to shape how we understand open education. The chapters in this part call for a greater focus on the capacity of open online courses to encompass difference. **Massiveness is more than learning at scale: it also brings complexity and diversity**.

Third, aspects of open courses are connected to the routines of data collection and processing that underpin the technologies involved in delivering them. Drawing on the critiques of instrumentalism in education technology discussed in part I and on emerging work in critical algorithm studies, this analysis highlights the ways analytic technologies are deeply entangled in educational practice and learner activity. We argue that the opaque inner world of algorithmic operations recenters educational power and agency through a kind of technoscientific governance. **Algorithms and analytics recode education: pay attention!**

Finally, this part examines the increasing automation of educational activity, and specifically teaching, through the use of data-driven technologies. Automation is examined as a key site for critical attention, given the prevailing economic rationale underpinning the notion of replacing particular teaching functions with precise and efficient machines described in part I. However, we also suggest that automation, used carefully, has the potential to offer a new source of critical, creative pedagogy, where alternative approaches built around the possibilities of excess and playful critique can be explored. **Automation need not impoverish education: we welcome our new robot colleagues.**

11

OPENNESS IS NEITHER NEUTRAL NOR NATURAL: IT CREATES AND DEPENDS ON CLOSURES.

The open education movement is both high profile and widely spread, yet definitions for just what *open* might mean in the context of education remain multiple, encompassing technical specifications for accessibility (Wiley 2014), licensing requirements for educational materials (Creative Commons, n.d.), the establishment of scholarly networks (Stewart 2015), or the community-building activities of lifelong learners (Bali et al. 2015). These various perspectives are regularly collected together under a general category of open education, in which openness often tends to be portrayed as a general condition that can endure over time, as well as migrate across geographical distances. However, important questions about the limits of the term remain. For example, in what sense can we understand education to *become* open and to remain so over time? How can the open education movement be considered global, that is, to span various continents with a unified idea of openness? These dilemmas relate directly to the practical concerns of how to design or teach an open course, where important decisions need to be made about the character and extent of the openness one might structure into the organization of resources or the arrangement of pedagogical activities.

Without a careful consideration of the meaning of openness, it is difficult to discern exactly what the condition of open education might be. The open education movement in general has tended to lack consistent theoretical foundations (Deimann and Farrow 2013; Oliver 2015), tacitly relying on what Knox (2013a) has framed as a negative rather than a positive form of openness. This draws on Isaiah Berlin's two concepts of liberty, where the positive form is described as a "freedom *to*" and the negative form as a "freedom *from*" in which the "defence of liberty consists in the 'negative' goal of warding off interference" (Berlin 1969, 60). In other words, a negative view of liberty, or indeed openness, tends to be concerned with the removal of perceived obstacles or barriers rather than on the characteristics of the resulting condition.

As Knox (2013a) shows, the open education movement has predominantly framed its mission in terms of freedom from, characterizing established educational institutions as rigid, antiquated, inaccessible, and ultimately closed, in opposition to which the open movement is cast as a disruptive liberation. Chief among the common economic arguments for open education has been that demand for higher education exceeds supply (Atkins, Brown, and Hammond 2007; Brown and Adler 2008; Laurillard 2008; Macintosh McGreal, and Taylor 2011; Daniel and Killion 2012), foregrounding geographical distance and financial cost as the principal barriers to openness in the sector. Elsewhere, Atkins et al. (2007) are more explicit about "the removal of 'unfreedoms'" (2007, 1), suggesting rather precisely the framing of open education in oppositional and negative terms, and largely failing to define any condition of ensuing openness. The assumption underpinning this—problematic in our view—is that if we continue focusing on the dismantling of obstacles, a liberating form of open education cannot fail to emerge.

Such overemphasis on the circumstances through which openness might emerge—that is, the removal of perceived barriers and the creation of backdrops into which projects can be situated—tends to result in two problematic and interrelated assumptions about the "open" of open education: that it is a straightforward, impartial condition and that it will emerge automatically once the right conditions are established. In other words, open education is neutral and natural.

As Caswell et al. (2008) emphasize, the right to education has long been established under article 26 of the Universal Declaration of Human Rights, for which open educational resources constitute the "movement to make this happen" (x). This association serves to naturalize the idea of open education as a core human entitlement; however, it also alludes to the particular kind of individualism that often underpins and inflects much of the discourse in this area. In foregrounding the idea of self-directing learners and diminishing the role of the institution and the professionalism of its teachers (see Knox 2013a, 2013b), open educational initiatives have tended to align themselves with the "learnification" described in part I of this book, which is problematic in the way it reduces the project of education entirely to the notion of learning and the learner (Biesta 2005, 2012).

Key to this shift is the framing of a transactional model for education, in which learners are cast as self-governing consumers of educational services (Biesta 2005). Trends for openness (especially MOOCs) have too often been subsumed into this neoliberal vision for the higher education sector (Hall 2015). Returning to Berlin's (1969) concept of negative liberty, one can discern the foundations of this political perspective as a curtailing of the centralized state to a role of defending individual freedoms, without which proponents claim "civilization cannot advance; the truth will not, for lack of a free market in ideas, come to light" (Berlin 1969, 60). This maps quite precisely to the position adopted by the open education movement, where the individual right to learn, and to learn more "authentically," must be served by diminishing institutional apparatus. The kind of institutionalized educational framing that might structure how learning should best come about is seen as an external imposition on the free market tendencies of self-directing and self-knowing learner-citizens. In this sense, we might better understand openness not as a straightforward, impartial, or neutral condition for education, but rather as one that is indicative of a particular political project of education, grounded in the idea of the individual as inherently motivated and independently able to "learn."

As Berlin (1969) astutely notes, one of the problems with an overemphasis on individual rights is a logical predisposition to overlook questions of power. This is precisely what Berlin means when he suggests of negative freedom that "liberty in this sense is principally concerned with the area of control, not with its source" (62). The area of control is the human subject (the self), and in the negative position, questions about its liberation far outweigh any interest in where or in what form liberation might be derived. In focusing on the rights and permissions of individuals, the open education movement has tended to devote less attention to the specific conditions of openness or to asking questions about how and from where it is produced and therefore what issues of authority, control, or privilege might be involved. One key example is the high-profile promotion of open educational resources (OER) as the technical solution to the training of a global workforce (Daniel and Killion 2012). Where Daniel and Killion write, "Imagine what our global economy will look like when the estimated 90% or more of earth's inhabitants currently locked out of high-quality post-secondary education and job training opportunities finally get a fair shot," the broader political and economic drivers of this brand of open education seem barely disguised. While it may be reasonable to assume a certain level of emancipatory transformation for many of these earthly inhabitants, there is also need to look at the kind of education on offer beyond simply the individual right to access. We need to look toward the underlying source of, and motivations for, this neoliberal vision of openness and question who might ultimately benefit from the resulting proliferation of human capital.

What is perhaps most important about this example is the exclusion of these potential trainees from established forms of education, of which formal teaching is perhaps the most conspicuous. Questions must be asked about the extent to which such ambitious projects infer a two-tier system, where the exclusivity of traditional institutions is maintained and the less fortunate must accept a teacherless model of self-direction. Crucially, however, it is a general sense of exclusion that must be underscored rather than necessarily the specifics of Daniel and Killion's (2012) OER example. In seeking to foster a seemingly unrestricted time and space for open education to occur, the open education movement tends to portray openness as an absolute, independent condition, in and of itself, that can serve as a normative goal for the project of education (Camilleri, Ehlers, and Pawlowski 2014)—in other words, the notion that educational activities, events, and organizations can be open, wholly, without being anything else.

Snapshot

Following the celebratory Year of Open in 2017, in 2018 the OEC announced the Open Education Awards for Excellence winners, conferring accolades on ten projects in the categories of open resources, tools, and practices (Open Education Consortium 2018). Particularly notable on this list is the winner of the Open Innovation prize: the OER World Map project, funded by the Hewlett Foundation (OER World Map, n.d.). Seeking to map a broad range of international OERs, the stated goal of the project is to "accelerate the evolution of the global OER ecosystem by providing a comprehensive and responsive picture of the OER movement." The picture, as one might expect, is a slick visualization featuring what appears to be a standard Mercator projection world map, with location markers that indicate a particular organization, service, individual, project, event, story, tool, or publication associated with OER. The list is as wide ranging as the world view itself, and the project emphasizes its "broad and inclusive approach" to what "belongs" on the map, as well as encouraging contributions and community participation. Claiming to connect stakeholders, provide statistics, and support policymakers, the OER World Map positions itself as "a kind of 'operations room' for the open education community." Important questions might be asked here about how such a broad collection of actors and activities has been categorized and homogenized: What is the definition of *openness* under which all these projects, in all their apparent diversity, sit? While more recent ventures appear to demonstrate an interest in the diversity of regional approaches, such as the Open Education Europa portal and the European MOOC aggregator EMMA, or national initiatives, such as XuetangX in China, the common ground here appears to be the homogenizing and universalizing notion of a global revolution (Cape Town Open Education Declaration 2007).

A more in-depth examination of openness should demonstrate that any notion of open is structurally tied to the notion of closed. As Edwards contends, "Openness is not the opposite of closed-ness, nor is there simply a continuum between the two." Rather, "All forms of openness entail forms of closedness and it is only through certain closings that certain openings become possible and vice versa" (Edwards 2015, 253). Instead of assuming that a natural condition of open learning exists beneath the inaccessible and exclusive infrastructures of university education, to be realized only if we were to dismantle them, the open education movement might rather recognize that openness does not overcome occlusion but rather "reconfigure[s] its possibilities" (Edwards 2015, 255). A key example here is research from early platform MOOCs, which were found to be populated by participants who already had experience of higher education rather than the supposedly marginalized populations claimed in much of the promotional discourse (Fischer 2014). In other words, the kind of openness offered by these platforms worked for particular groups of people and not others; those with access to the required technology, as well as the experience and confidence to learn independently. Despite the claims of a unified movement of openness, open education projects are better understood as a much more complex, multiple, and conflicted arrangement that simultaneously opens certain opportunities for engagement while closing off others. As such, they are inherently political.

Our manifesto point therefore aims to suggest that the open education movement could do more to recognize and engage with these critical perspectives on the notion of open. While Oliver (2015) has specifically suggested the reframing of open education in terms of "positive liberty," there is also a growing interest in open educational practice, which calls for a shift to the consideration of pedagogical activity and routines rather than resources and materials (see Cronin and MacLaren 2018). Important work here has considered the extent to which open education programs have addressed social justice issues in developing contexts (Hodgkinson-Williams and Trotter 2018), as well as proposed pedagogical design specifically for educational equity, alongside open access (Kalir 2018). A key aspect of this work is the surfacing of marginalized and minority perspectives, too often overlooked in the more mainstream advocacy of open education. As such, these perspectives are more overtly concerned with how a present openness might function through education, as opposed to a focus on the absence of barriers to accessing educational content. Such perspectives do important work in foregrounding the complexity of openness and creating a positive future direction for research that engages the manifesto point extended here: **Openness is neither neutral nor natural: it creates and depends on closures.**

12

MASSIVENESS IS MORE THAN LEARNING AT SCALE: IT ALSO BRINGS COMPLEXITY AND DIVERSITY.

The lack of boundaries around the definition of open education has given rise to all kinds of broadly open projects and initiatives, the best known of which is undoubtedly the MOOC, online courses attracting high numbers of participants, often providing free or low-cost access to materials and resources. In particular, the MOOC platform organizations achieved such prominence around 2012 to 2014 that they appeared in some instances to substitute for the broader open education movement itself. Propelling the notion of open education into the mainstream, the MOOC platforms, as some have argued, wrote their own histories to legitimize their position as originators of the movement (Watters 2015), neglecting to make reference to earlier experiments in connectivist learning (see McAuley et al. 2010). It is to the MOOC platforms in particular that we now turn.

Structured courses, as opposed to collections of resources, have been a significant feature of open education, often as part of an effort to align openness with formal education. MOOCs achieved particular prominence from 2012 onward, intensifying discussions of accessibility and scale in the higher education sector. Sharing territory with the OER World Map, various studies have represented the impact of MOOCs through world map visualizations (Perna et al. 2013; Breslow et al. 2013), creating a similar kind of spatiotemporal context from which the relevance and scale of these courses have been rationalized. Notions of high student demand and large class sizes accompanied MOOC promotion from the offset. The flurry of media attention around the launch of Stanford University's Introduction to Artificial Intelligence in 2011 established the trend, with the *New York Times* foregrounding enrollment numbers (at that time 58,000) in the title of a piece that emphasized the implications of "a class nearly four times the size of Stanford's entire student body" (Markoff 2011). The capacity to accommodate large numbers of students has thus been a defining characteristic of MOOC platforms and has granted them a high level of media interest largely unseen in other areas of online education innovation. Interest in the numbers of students participating in MOOCs remains fervent, with the latest report at the time of writing from Class Central, a MOOC search engine, suggesting 101 million enrollments from 2011 to 2018 (Shah 2018a). As well as defining the format, massive enrollments appear to determine the success of the MOOC venture, as recent concerns over a "serious decline" in enrollments on the edX MOOC platform might suggest (Coldewey 2017). In order for MOOCs to remain MOOCs, it appears, high numbers of enrollments must be maintained.

Enrollment numbers have been key to the promotion of the MOOC because they promise to address two key narratives in contemporary discourse around higher education:

an increasing demand for provision, often linked to so-called Global South populations, and greater efficiency in the delivery of teaching. Reports such as the sensationally titled *An Avalanche Is Coming* from the Institute for Public Policy Research depict the global demand for higher education as potentially catastrophic, alleviated substantially by the supposed disruption and unbundling brought about by MOOCs and other innovations (Barber, Donnelly, and Rizvi 2013). The central justification here, repeated all too frequently in media reporting (Enbar 2016), is that the higher education system is malfunctioning and in desperate need of profound transformation. Entangled with the narrative of increasing demand is the framing of traditional educational organizations as grossly inefficient. While much was made of the appeal of well-known Stanford professors Peter Norvig and Sebastian Thurn in the Introduction to Artificial Intelligence MOOC (Matson 2011), the underlying message was one of efficiency. Later enrollments in this MOOC were reported at over 120,000, seeming to indicate astonishingly productive ratios between teachers and students. More recent figures from individual MOOCs suggest two examples of courses with over 1 million enrollments (Online Course Report 2017).

With such numbers, it is perhaps easy to perceive the intoxicating appeal of MOOC teaching, where pedagogical activity is neatly captured through the video lecture and broadcast to vast populations of eager learners. However, this arrangement constitutes a fairly radical shift in what one might assume to be a more traditional relationship between teacher and student—one where direct contact is possible, and desirable, and where there is at least some capacity for teacher-student interaction. The economy achieved by the extraordinary scale

of MOOC provision results in what would appear to be surface, if not superficial, encounters between the teacher and
the taught. As such, research has highlighted passive behaviors in MOOC participants (Milligan and Littlejohn 2014), and
questions have been raised about the isolation of students in
such courses (Bayne, Knox, and Ross 2015). As Stewart (2013)
identifies, the notion of scale in MOOCs is predominantly an
economic one, based on "the premise of repeatable processes
delivering identical products or services" (231). This encapsu-
lates the excitement around MOOC enrollments rather well,
where a single set of digitized course materials can be replicated, for all intents and purposes, indefinitely.

However, identifying the assumptions that underpin this
vision of openness is key to developing a critical understanding of the scaled provision of the MOOC. Returning to the
work of Isaiah Berlin, one might identify the MOOC as a prime
example of the promotion of open education as freedom from.
The two central narratives here—the increasing demand for
higher education and greater efficiency in teaching—align
directly with the barriers regularly described by MOOC proponents: a lack of physical access to an educational institution, as well as the absence of financial means to do so. There
are not enough higher education institutions, the argument
goes, within reasonable proximity of the majority of potential
students, and that majority is not able to meet the significant
cost of participating. This has been the foundation of the promotional machinery employed by the platform organizations,
often overtly framing the MOOC project as the educational
emancipation of a non-Western audience (Knox 2016a).

Importantly, however, underpinning this simplistic vision of
open education as the removal of geographical and economic

obstacles, as well as the one-directional economy of scale in the MOOC, are problematic assumptions about the kinds of learners participating in them. Where the endless replication of educational content is the core delivery model, those on the receiving end of MOOC delivery are cast as a culturally and socially homogeneous population inhabiting a universal world characterized by the presence of large numbers of students already educated enough to make self-directed participation possible. In classes of hundreds of thousands, there appears to be little to indicate the profound diversity that exists in the international populations of the MOOC. Adam (2019) provides an important critique of the digital neocolonialism of MOOCs here, suggesting that such endeavors "not only need to cater for difference in their conceptualisation of learners in terms of geographical and infrastructural contexts, but also create room for inclusion of different ways of thinking, knowing, and being" (377).

While MOOCs can therefore be seen as instilling a form of standardization—significantly at the international rather than the merely national scale—this should be understood as informed by a core commitment to a particular view of the kind of participants involved. While the early promotion of the platform MOOCs made more explicit claims about the appeal of their courses to supposed non-Western populations (see Knox 2017a), subsequent research revealed much more significant participation from those with already established access to higher education and few enrollments from, for example, Africa (Perna et al. 2013). Seven years after the launch of Introduction to Artificial Intelligence, the MOOC landscape appears a lot more complex than the media interest tended to portray at that time. The MOOC platforms have developed their services toward monetization rather than the initial emphasis on free access. Recent developments such as the MicroMasters programs from edX foreground industry endorsement and offer credentials that can contribute to a full master's degree (EdX, n.d.a). Coursera offers a similar service, under the trademarked name MasterTrack (Shah 2018b). Such course completion, edX suggests, happens "whenever and wherever you choose—this is mastery made flexible!" These are concerted initiatives to decentralize and unbundle traditional credentialing systems, and they are importantly underpinned and justified by the figure of a learner who is able to make choices and to govern his or her own educational trajectory with little or no teacher guidance. The population assumed to be demanding the MOOC brand of higher education therefore appears to be distinctly neoliberal in character, with the platform organizations apparently working to diminish potential infringements on the flourishing of self-directing individuals in part by sidelining the teacher.

The problem with this framing of the MOOC is that the notion of the rational learner, rather than any educational rationale, becomes the central focus. In other words, as Biesta discusses (2005), the broader focus on learning and the learner, as opposed to education and teaching, tends to suppress important questions about the purpose of education (see part I for a fuller discussion of learnification). Where the desires and motivations of the individual become the guiding principles for the MOOC model, little attention is given to the broader, overarching justification for the kind of education on offer. MicroMasters programs, or indeed the prevalence of business and technology courses on the MOOC platforms—by far the largest categories, at 18.2 percent and 20.4 percent, respectively (Shah 2018a)—come about because they are perceived to be a response to student demand, not because there is any underlying rationale for why such an education is beneficial, beyond the economic one.

So who are these learner-consumers who appear to be in the driver's seat when it comes to the development of the MOOC? While the traditional undergraduate university student isn't quite the rational, self-directed embodiment of human capital that the platform organizations cater to, the "professional learner" appears to fit the mold more precisely. As Rick Levin (2017), former CEO of Coursera, outlined in his keynote address to the EMOOCs conference in 2017—entitled "Five Years after the Year of the MOOC: Where Are We Now?"—89 percent of the platform's learner population were over twenty-two years of age, and 45 percent were from emerging economies. This is, it would therefore seem, a population already within employment, or at least beyond formal schooling, who perceive the MOOC not as the grand formative experience of education but rather as specific and focused vocational training. In this sense, any notion of student demand is also necessarily characterized by the inclination and ability to pay for MOOC services. As Shah explains in reference to the dominance of business and technology subjects across the MOOC platforms, they are "the categories that are the easiest to monetize" (Shah 2018a). As such, the credentialing that MOOC platforms is increasingly shifting toward is gaining currency first and foremost among employers, not necessarily educational institutions (Levin 2017).

The all-encompassing corporate vision for the future of education that characterized early MOOC publicity (Knox 2016a) appears to have refashioned the format in its own image. The heady promotion of The Year of the MOOC (Pappano 2012), which included Coursera founder Daphne's Koller's (2012) allusions to solving the tragic consequences of stampedes for university places in South Africa, or Udacity founder Sebastian Thrun's (see Leckart 2012) dramatic claims of a future with only ten higher education institutions, now seems crude and outdated. However, there was something in this early ambition and idealism, however exaggerated, that has ultimately been lost. Principally, the early discussions of massive enrollments offered a glimpse of tangible opportunities to explore the challenges of global education as a project of engaging with difference, an alternative to the drive for repetition and curricular conformity now manifest in the economies of scale of the MOOC platforms. As Simon Nelson (2017), CEO of FutureLearn, makes clear, the platform's strategy is now one of "returning value to partners" and opening new markets rather than any notion of disrupting or opening up the university system. As such, one might argue that the elitism and exclusivity of established educational institutions are maintained much more than they are unsettled; the disruption occurs merely at the level of admission to learning experiences already defined by an increasingly marketized higher education sector.

We talk about the engagement with difference here as a way of suggesting that there are more structural and critical shifts that could arise from the kind of massive activity promised by the MOOC. Aside from our own E-learning and Digital Cultures course on Coursera, which encouraged participation outside the platform (see Knox 2016a), there are other examples of MOOCs that offer modes of participation and curricula that appear to work with, rather than against, the complexity and diversity of the global classroom. One example of a platform-based MOOC that has grounded its design and pedagogical practices around local, self-organizing groups (so-called hubs) and synchronous online sessions rather than the typical broadcast pedagogy of other platforms is u.lab: Leading from the Emerging Future (EdX, n.d.b). Working with a much more complex online and offline arrangement, the MOOC is suggested to be "a vehicle for massive open civic engagement and cross-sectoral change" (Sharmer 2017) as opposed to vocational training and is concerned with "the transformation of capitalism itself" (edX 2014). While such grand visions might be seen as a return to the hyperbolic tendencies of the early days of the MOOC, there appears to be a much clearer engagement with the idea of global educational activity than in the more established platform model of scaled university provision.

Other important developments demonstrate a challenge to the easy categorization of MOOCs, through which the grouping and sorting of students, as well as the demarcation and maintenance of perceived disciplinary boundaries, are amplified. Scientific Humanities, led by philosopher and anthropologist Bruno Latour and delivered on the France Université Numérique (FUN) platform (FUN-MOOC, n.d.a), is one example of a MOOC established around interdisciplinary work. Exploring the field of science and technology studies, the course promises to "equip future citizens with the means to be at ease with many issues that straddle the distinctions between science, morality, politics and society" (FUN-MOOC, n.d.b). Appearing to acknowledge the propensity for disagreement as much as consensus in open classrooms, the course claims to allow participants to "handle the flood of different opinions about contentious issues." With the motto *cogitamus ergo civitas sumus* (We think, thus we form a collective together), Scientific Humanities appears to embrace and foreground the kinds of challenges glossed over by the individualized activities and neatly packaged curricula of more established MOOC offers. Vital work is also emerging to connect postcolonial perspectives with the project of the MOOC, revealing not only a distinct lack of current engagement with non-Western knowledge and educational practice, but also tangible ways of including marginalized voices and developing a plurality of knowledge (see Bali and Sharma 2017; Adam 2019). Rather than rehearsing, broadcasting, and amplifying existing university curricula, this work calls for MOOCs to acknowledge and incorporate the global reach of their educational activities in an effort to attempt to draw the diverse cultural practices and understandings of their participants into the formal curricula of the institution. **Massiveness is more than learning at scale: it also brings complexity and diversity.**

13

ALGORITHMS AND ANALYTICS RECODE EDUCATION: PAY ATTENTION!

The MOOCs we have discussed have been linked in our research with notions of "data colonialism" (Knox 2016a), a critical perspective that highlights the bias and discrimination apparent in the technologies at work beneath the slick facades of course software. It is to these considerations we now turn.

Perhaps one of the most surprising aspects of projects to develop learning at scale is the lack of attention given to the technology that makes such global education possible. Platform promotion has tended to describe the MOOC, for example, simply as a means of access, or a "transparent window" to universities (Knox 2016b, 311), and research has been largely focused around student retention (Jordan 2014; Henderikx, Kreijns, and Kalz 2017), or broad demographics (Breslow et al. 2013; Perna et al. 2013). The focus on removing barriers to participation seems to overlook the significant transformation of education brought about by the vastly complex technological infrastructure and software involved in offering courses online. Through this point in the manifesto, we argue that it is important to understand the move online as a recoding, a transformation, rather than an augmentation or, indeed, enhancement of education. New technologies change and reshape what we do as teachers—sometimes for better, sometimes for worse—regardless of how often we prefer to speak of them as enhancements or tools.

In line with the sociomaterial perspective we have applied throughout this book, educational technology should be understood not simply as a set of tools applied to an existing and authentic education, but as formative of, and inextricable from, the educational contexts in which it is involved. However, casting the MOOC—for example—as the ultimate freedom *from* obstacles to access is directly premised on the assumption of technology as neutral, straightforwardly providing a way in to a supposedly unchanged educational experience. It is important, then, to understand much of the discourse around open and online education as lacking in theoretical engagement with the active role of technology; it either ignores it or describes it in terms that are "rooted in a kind of mad instrumentalized culture of positivism and technological rationality" (Giroux 2017, 141).

However, recent developments in learning analytics (see Lang et al. 2017) are surfacing tangible examples of technologies— involved in identifying at-risk students, or automating teacher feedback—that challenge this apparent neutrality, and the MOOC has been a significant player in the emergence of such approaches in education. This is largely because of the large numbers of new kinds of participants taking MOOCs, which have generated the kind of sizable data sets needed to drive analytic modeling. Learning analytics is typically defined as "measurement, collection, analysis and reporting of data about learners and their contexts, for purposes of understanding and optimising learning and the environments in which it occurs" (Long and Siemens 2011, 34).

Beginning with this definition, two important and interrelated issues become apparent with respect to the idea that this technology recodes education: first, in the sense of the discursive shifts that have come to prominence as learning analytics gains traction in the sector and, second, in relation to the concrete ways learning analytics software is able to produce environments that directly influence educational activities and shape learners through automation. This has implications for the understanding of education in its capacity to liberate, as well as for assumptions about the kinds of subjectivity attributed to students, as has been discussed previously in relation to the work of Isaiah Berlin.

A flourishing area of research has developed around the Society for Learning Analytics Research (SoLAR, n.d.), including a program of summer institutes and international conferences and the establishment of a dedicated academic journal (*Journal of Learning Analytics*). As an emergent field, learning analytics has garnered significant attention, including influential reports from Universities UK (2016) and the development of institutional policy (see Tsai and Gasevic 2017). Analytics are becoming common within the day-to-day experience of teachers and students, increasingly appearing in the form of dashboards as educational software companies and platforms develop their products (Clow 2013). Horizon scanning in higher education has frequently forecast the imminent disruption of teaching and learning practices through such additions (Johnson et al. 2014, 2015, 2016).

Paying attention to this body of work reveals important ways in which education is being reframed and recoded, in particular in relation to the role of the teacher. Advocates of learning analytics promote notions of "actionable intelligence" (Campbell, De Blois, and Oblinger 2007) and "data driven decision making" (Barneveld, Arnold, and Campbell 2012), which appear to clearly position analytics as providing an objective basis for subsequent educational intervention. This holds the potential to give precedence and authority to the insights generated through the data dashboard over those of the human teacher, who is often positioned merely to respond to analytic outputs (Knox 2017b).

This can be understood as an extension of the teacherless model of student self-direction discussed earlier in relation to open education. It is a kind of mythologizing of the objectivity of data (boyd and Crawford 2012) introduced to supplant the supposed deficiencies and inefficiencies of human teachers. This assumed need to supplement the capacities of the teacher partly derives from the convergence, through learning analytics, of particular kinds of disciplinary expertise in the educational environment. While learning analytics software is designed for end use by teachers, students, and educational administrators, it draws from highly specific techniques developed from data mining and business intelligence (Ferguson 2012). In this sense, it can be understood as black-boxed technology (Latour 1999), encouraging engagement with its outputs—in the form of dashboards and visualizations—but concealing the complexity of its functioning, which is incomprehensible to those without proficiency in data science.

Through learning analytics, therefore, pedagogic authority and the capacity to make decisions about the activity and progress of learners is being spread across humans and machines, and strongly inflected by data science practices and expertise.

This is not necessarily problematic—in fact, interdisciplinary partnerships are essential to the future of educational research and development—but it becomes so where teachers and the act of teaching are not placed at the center of the design and development of new educational technologies and where the supposed objectivity of data is not subjected to critical interrogation by educators themselves.

This relates to a second, and equally important, aspect of learning analytics, which involves a more literal recoding of the educational environment through the deployment of data and algorithm. Sociological studies are beginning to pay attention to the "algorithmic culture" (Striphas 2015) emerging from the increasing prevalence of complex computational routines in "social ordering, governance and control" (Williamson 2014). Algorithms are becoming "powerful and consequential actors in a wide variety of domains" (Ziewitz 2015, 3). While a technical description of an algorithm might suggest simply the "encoded procedures for transforming input data into a desired output, based on specified calculations" (Gillespie 2014, 167), critical work in this area is developing a much broader and complex picture of the social power of the algorithm (Beer 2017), and its involvement in the "proceduralisation of knowledge, and as a result, the formalizing and delineating of social life" (Knox 2018, 165). It is important, then, to understand algorithms in relation to the broader social systems in which they operate rather than simply as isolated technical operations or encoded instructions. The technical definition of the algorithm overlooks the powerful ways in which these highly complex routines are often deeply enmeshed in human activities. They are shaped and defined through user interactions, but also work to shape and define users, through ordering, recommending, disclosing, or concealing information.

Important work is examining the biases generated through algorithmic systems, such as problematic profiling in the prediction of recidivism and, notably for this discussion, the gaming of university rankings (O'Neil 2016). As Knox (2018) demonstrates, algorithms are increasingly being used in MOOCs to, for example, intervene in learning activities or categorize learners into particular groups. Algorithms can therefore be understood to actively construct social relations, as much as objectively measure them through technical procedures. It is algorithms that often operate beneath the surface of learning analytics systems, as performative devices that produce rather than discover educational realities through techniques such as cluster analysis (see Perrotta and Williamson 2018). Understood as recodings, these techniques produce powerful and convincing outcomes that are beginning to shape educational policy (Williamson 2017). In this sense, it is important to understand algorithms in material terms, as concrete actors interwoven in the fabric of educational activity, influencing and shaping both governance and practice. The capacity for analytics and their underlying algorithms to efficiently process large volumes of data and provide empirical and tangible outcomes is key to understanding their appeal in an education system eager not only for economical solutions but also for decisive measures. In this way, analytics and algorithms might be seen as not only aligned with but also as amplifying "the logic of economic rationality and 'accountability' that pervades governance cultures in education" (Perrotta and Williamson 2018, 4).

While it might be tempting to view analytics and algorithms as straightforwardly liberating—unburdening teachers and administrators of the difficult task of identifying which students are failing or delivering students from states of incomprehension about their performance—a more critical perspective is needed, one that recognizes an intensification of technocratic control in education. On the one hand, the dashboards and visualizations generated by learning analytics offer an unprecedented, and alluring, appearance of transparency in the often complicated, obscure, and intangible domain of learning. On the other hand, the extent to which decision-making power is shifted away from teachers and students, and toward new kinds of data science expertise, needs further examination. Moreover, as emerging work outside education is highlighting, data-driven technologies are increasingly being employed in ways that amplify existing social inequalities (Eubanks 2018; Noble 2018), and more research is needed to investigate the ways in which educational analytics might replicate and intensify deeply embedded discrimination within our societies and our institutions. Prinsloo's (2016) suggestions for decolonizing the use of educational data offer one productive avenue of exploration here. The drive to collect, process, and analyze student data in education has the potential to embed an opaque inner world of algorithmic operations that centralizes educational power and agency through a kind of technoscientific governance that is directly at odds with teacher professionalism. As teachers and researchers, we need to build research programs and teaching methods that directly address this risk while remaining open to the many creative and potentially critical uses of computational data that are available to us. **Algorithms and analytics recode education: pay attention!**

14

AUTOMATION NEED NOT IMPOVERISH EDUCATION: WE WELCOME OUR NEW ROBOT COLLEAGUES.

Despite the powerful technoscientific recoding of the sector explored above, we argue that tangible opportunities remain for teachers to shape the agenda of algorithmic technologies in education. This chapter builds on the critique presented in chapter 13, addressing in further detail the topic of automation. It does this by attempting—perhaps surprisingly—to engage not just with its problematic aspects, but also by assessing some of the positive ways in which teachers might engage with the algorithmic and data-driven technologies of automation.

The automation of teaching has been a long-standing aim of for-profit technocorporations, technorationalist education management, and others seeing technology as an instrument for scaling up education with low-cost implications or achieving other efficiencies in existing education systems. It has for these reasons also been an enduring point of resistance for the profession, and a highly politicized trope within schools and institutions of higher learning. Dramatic accounts of the potential replacement of teachers by technology, in particular by artificial intelligence (AI) in a context of wider concerns around the future of work, surface periodically in education (von Radowitz 2017). Yet research and development to date has been directed more toward the incremental automation of specific teaching functions than of teachers themselves (plagiarism detection is one example, discussed in part V).

The manifesto point we address here is often commented on as sitting oddly with the generally critical focus of other aspects of the manifesto. Yet we argue that if we do not feel ready at this point to actively welcome our robot colleagues, we should at least be prepared to open the door to them. To the extent that aspects of automation may prove to be genuinely beneficial to teachers, it seems important to remain open to the idea that it may allow us to explore new kinds of critical pedagogies, new creative possibilities, and new kinds of usefulness to our students. The key point we wish to make here is that for this to be the case, research and development of automation technologies in teaching should not be developed for teachers but by teachers. Teachers, the act of teaching, and the learning and well-being of students, not efficiency imperatives or fantasies of frictionless scaling up of education, should be placed at the center of the way we think about automation.

Snapshot

One example, focused on the automation of tutor feedback, is OnTask, a system developed by the University of Sydney. OnTask is described as a "software tool that gathers and assesses data about students' activities throughout the semester" (OnTask 2019), allowing teachers to design personalized feedback that is released to students automatically, based on these mapped activities.

Data are collected from a range of sources, including course engagement, assessments, student information systems, and discussion forums. Feedback points are determined by teachers, and feedback is written (again by teachers) for a range of types of student activity (for example, if a student hasn't posted in a forum for a given period of time, or has posted but not commented on others' posts, or has not engaged with a critical part of the course). In this way, the system promises to allow teachers to "connect large data sets about students with concrete and frequent actions to support their learning" (OnTask 2019).

OnTask supports teachers in writing and delivering feedback to large cohorts of students and is able to address a variety of student behaviors and scenarios. Critically, its use is designed to be tightly aligned to the structure of the course it is being used within, and feedback messages to students are written directly by teachers. In this way, it aims to avoid being a faceless system based on generic data or messages, and there is a greater chance that feedback is appropriate and well aligned. In this way, it promises to increase teacher visibility in large courses in a positive way. Rather than undermine the professionalism of the teacher, it could be argued that it provides teachers with a different—and arguably even more professionalized—way to enact a highly expert set of practices.

Two driving ideas tend to underpin the push for automation of aspects of teaching: the aim of providing personalized, direct student-to-teacher tuition and the commitment to efficient pedagogic delivery. Crucially, both of these ideas reveal underlying assumptions about the relationships between humans and technologies that tend to limit the ways automation manifests in educational practices. The narrative of personalization is particularly prominent here, where data-driven algorithmic technologies are promoted as ways of tailoring educational content or feedback for an individual student. This idea has attracted significant interest—or example, in the form of funding from the Gates Foundation (Newton 2016) and the development of the Personalized Learning Plan software associated with Facebook (Herold 2016). Underlying this work is often an explicit aim of producing a personalized, one-to-one tutor for every student using automated, artificially intelligent, and data-driven technology. Prominent educational commentator Sir Anthony Seldon has promoted this idea, suggesting "the possibility of an Eton or Wellington education for all" through the idea that "'everyone can have the very best teacher' driven by 'adaptive machines that adapt to individuals'" (von Radowitz 2017). Milena Marinova, director of artificial intelligence at educational publisher Pearson, appears to share this vision, describing an idealized world of educational AI in which "every student would have that Aristotle tutor, that one-on-one, and every teacher would know everything there is to know about every subject" (see Olson 2018). This is a fantasy that extends back decades, to the early years of educational technology, when Patrick Suppes (1966) predicted that "in a few more years millions of school children will have access to what Philip of Macedon's son Alexander enjoyed as a royal prerogative: the personal services of a tutor as well-informed and responsive as Aristotle" (207).

As Friesen (2019) elaborates, the ideal of the one-to-one personal tutor is a well-established and orthodox basis for education, stretching back through Rousseau, Comenius, and Socrates (through Plato and Xenophon). Rather than being straightforwardly innovative, the automated tutor manifests as a "a kind of repetitive continuity" (4). For Friesen, the promise of the automated AI tutor can be understood as part of a contemporary "technological imaginary" of the global availability of learning (Friesen 2019, 2). Friesen further questions the "mythology" of the one-to-one educational relationship, and the way it has been taken up by computing science as representative of an authentic form of pedagogy. For Friesen, "dialogue, in short, is a ubiquitous yet irreducible experience" (2019, 12), and attempts to replicate it with technical systems merely produce systems of control: "For education or any other aspect of social activity to fall so completely under the dominance of a total vision of social and technical engineering would be 'totalitarian' in and of itself" (13).

Automating technologies adopt computing and data science methods that tend to be oriented toward the categorization of individual students and predefinition of possible routes through supposedly personalized environments. In this sense, they codify and systematize educational conversations and relationships that are generally seen by teachers themselves as more malleable and emergent. As we have suggested, an economic rationale tends to underpin the development of such systems, which position automation as a way of introducing efficiency into teaching practice. This drives the idea that automation provides a straightforward labor-saving function that can free teachers from the routine and repetitive aspects of teaching and create space for the nurturing of abilities assumed to be uniquely human in both teachers and students.

Phillips (2018), for example, sees data-driven technologies, such as machine learning and AI, as having the ability to diminish "the mundane duties that consume a teacher's time," notably here singling out "grading papers and tests" as examples of the banal tasks of the teaching profession (Phillips 2018). Key to this rationale is the idea that a more authentic mode of teaching can be achieved once teachers are liberated from such burdens, with technological development—rather than, for example, a rethinking of the way we approach assessment and grading—seen as the solution. Extolling the virtues of artificial intelligence in education (or "AIEd"), Luckin et al. (2016) suggest: "Freedom from routine, time-consuming tasks will allow teachers to devote more of their energies to the creative and very human acts that provide the ingenuity and empathy needed to take learning to the next level" (31).

This is a key aspect of the discourse around automation in education, which positions the technology as passive and instrumental while portraying teaching and learning as creative, entrepreneurial, and, ultimately, more authentically human. Distinguishing a specific role and set of capacities for humans using automated technologies is well established, with Moffatt and Rich (1957) suggesting that a future society is "likely to put a premium on originative skill and imagination" (273).

It is not just teachers therefore who benefit from the supposed ability of automated technologies to render humans "more human." Luckin et al. (2016) frame AIEd as specifically designed to provide the means through which students can unleash their intelligence, directed toward particular ideas about the kinds of skills and abilities required for a future world of pervasive automation. Employment in this scenario will be more "cognitively demanding," necessitating the "higher order skills" of problem solving (47). This labor will also involve "social skills . . . [the] ability to get on with others, to empathise and create a human connection" (47). Such abilities are seen as emanating at least in part from a structured personalization and a one-to-one relationship with the technology.

What we find across the calls for personalization and labor-saving automation in education is a prominent turn toward a broader discussion of the human condition and the ways it might be differentiated from the emergence of ever smarter technologies. The place of the learner is apparently prioritized over the workings of the technology in this vision, yet the supposedly human qualities on which learner preeminence is based are thinly defined. Moreover, this attention to the quality of the human condition should be seen as a long-standing educational orthodoxy rather than some new direction for teaching in an era of automation. As Pedersen (2015) reminds us, education has long been viewed as the "humanist project par excellence," seen as a "a key component of compulsory becoming-human . . . connected to a general idea of education as something inherently 'good,' that can somehow make us become better human beings."

This educational commitment to humanism is clearly maintained in the discourses of human exceptionalism that accompany the promotion of data-driven automation in education. However, as our own research has argued (Bayne 2015b), this perspective significantly limits the ways we as teachers can conceive of working with technologies in education by holding an authentic humanness separate from technical artifacts and tools. Much more creative and expansive opportunities arise when this underlying separation is challenged and a posthumanist sensitivity to the entangled relationships between humans and technologies is embraced (Bayne 2015b). (See part I of this book for an overview of this area of theory and its importance to the manifesto.)

In other words, rather than perceiving automated technologies as merely instrumental—passively delivering a personalized curriculum or straightforwardly contributing to imperatives for efficiency and scale—one might seek to surface

ways of bringing automation and pedagogy together in productive and playful relationships that develop teachers' and
students' critical understanding of digital education. Automated agents should not be developed only by data scientists.
If teachers can take control, shaping and forming automated
agencies that align with their own professional values, we open
up a future of critical and creative teaching that is far beyond
the instrumental assumptions, humanist orthodoxies, and
technocorporate visions of scale and efficiency which have
dominated the debate so far. **Automation need not impoverish education: we welcome our new robot colleagues.**

Snapshot

In 2014, we designed and deployed an automated "teacherbot"
system in order to critically and playfully experiment with co-
teaching methods in our own massive open online course (the
E-Learning and Digital Cultures MOOC). The teacherbot worked
within the Twitter feed for the course, allowing the teaching team
to predefine a number of automated responses to tweets triggered
by various key words. Students were aware that the teacherbot
was an automated presence in the course, and there was no intention to attempt to simulate human teacher presence (for a comparison, see the virtual teaching assistant developed at Georgia
Tech described by Goel and Polepeddi 2016). Rather than seeking to replace the human teachers or provide a flawless "better-
than-human" teacher, the teacherbot was designed as a way of
manifesting teaching activity as a messy assemblage of data, algorithms, and human agency.

Frequently, the teacherbot misinterpreted student tweets, but
these misunderstandings were also sometimes generative, surfacing a serendipity and unpredictability that enriched the communications and would have been lost with a more precise system.
Students regularly attempted to trick the bot with tweets intended

to test its abilities, actively exploring their own sense of human and machine boundaries. By centering the messy questions, dilemmas, and challenges of automation rather than smoothing them over with a veneer of precision, the teacherbot encouraged students to think more critically about the role of automated technologies in education and to consider how teachers and bots might work as collaborative pedagogical partners. (For a full description and analysis of the teacherbot, see Bayne 2016.)

CONCLUSION: THE POLITICS OF "TECHNICAL DISRUPTIONS"

This part has examined four prominent aspects of digital education signaled by four statements in the Manifesto for Teaching Online: open education, MOOCs, algorithms, and automation.

Openness is neither neutral nor natural: it creates and depends on closures.

Massiveness is more than learning at scale: it also brings complexity and diversity.

Algorithms and analytics recode education: pay attention!

Automation need not impoverish education: we welcome our new robot colleagues.

The sequence of these points is important, highlighting the ways that open education initiatives have been positioned within a wider shift toward data collection and the extraction of value through algorithmic processing. Both openness and automation have garnered much in the way of mainstream media attention in recent years, each seen as potentially transforming the higher education sector by breaking down barriers to participation and enhancing and economizing teaching practices. It is therefore vitally important to temper these high-profile discourses of disruption with teacher and teaching-centered perspectives that surface the ways in which they are problematic.

Drawing on the work of Isaiah Berlin's "Two Concepts of Liberty" (1969), we have seen that forms of open education often assume a political role aimed at reducing centralized barriers to access within a tacit understanding that openness is ideologically neutral. It assumes the presence of a body of learners who are already self-directing, autonomous, and independent thinkers. This kind of "negative openness" is inclined toward the view that the ability and desire to learn is instinctive and innate and will naturally emerge without the need to specify its operational details or ideological basis in advance. We counter this view with the point that the primary responsibility of education is to support students in the ability to think critically and independently; we cannot assume that these capacities are in some way preloaded and ready to go. We have therefore argued for the recognition of the complexity of the ideal of openness, suggesting that all openings create new closures. It is not sufficient to see openness as a transcendent, universal, and utopic condition by which education can be straightforwardly transformed.

The chapters in this part have also discussed the ways in which MOOCs emerged as a high-profile example of open education, promising liberation from the constraints of geographical distance and financial limitations, as well as the centralized curricular and pedagogic structures of university campuses. We have suggested that this view takes an overly narrow and uncritical view of participants as human capital, easing in new global forms of standardized and scaled pro-vision. Despite this, alternative MOOCs have emerged that demonstrate more interesting course designs that account for localized, self-organizing groups and open up new ways of understanding interdisciplinarity.

We have argued that attention needs to be paid to the grow-ing use of data-intensive computational processing in educa-tion. The burgeoning field of learning analytics is offering powerful and appealing insights about educational activity through software interfaces, dashboards, and visualizations. These technologies can be seen to call into question and shift the authority and professionalism of the teacher, while the emergent algorithmic infrastructure permeating contempo-rary educational activity is introducing a new kind of exclu-sive, centralized technocracy, impenetrable to students and teachers alike.

The chapters in part III have outlined some of the ways such data-driven technologies are being employed for auto-mating certain teaching functions. We outlined the historical drive for personalized learning and its underlying emphasis on efficiency and instrumentalism. Significantly, this discourse was shown to promote a particular view of humanness cata-lyzed as a way of preserving human exceptionality in a world of increasing automation. While the manifesto is concerned with encouraging critical perspectives on the rise of automated technologies in education, part of this involves opening up space to consider creative alternatives, so we also present some proposals for an automation that replaces efficiency and preci-sion with a playful kind of excess, demonstrating a way ahead that values the productive entanglement of human teachers and automated teaching machines.

IV

FACE, SPACE, AND PLACE

MANIFESTO POINTS COVERED

Online can be the privileged mode. Distance is a positive principle, not a deficit.

Contact works in multiple ways. Face time is overvalued.

Digital education reshapes its subjects. The possibility of the
"online version" is overstated.

Place is differently, not less, important online.

Distance is temporal, affective, political: not simply spatial.

Figure 4.1

INTRODUCTION

Part IV challenges perspectives that see online and, in particular, distance, education as structurally and pedagogically inferior to education that takes place on-campus or face-to-face. This discussion is framed by the overarching argument, set out in the chapter 15, that distance and online education is not the deficit mode it is often cast as—a second-best option for when embodied presence at a college or university is impossible. Rather, it is an opportunity for teachers and students to work with different forms and mediations of face, space, and place that have the potential to create better ways to do teaching and learning. **Online can be the privileged mode. Distance is a positive principle, not a deficit.**

Teachers who emphasize the value of teaching and learning on-campus, as opposed to learning in online spaces, often present compelling lists of the opportunities that traditional forms of engagement with students offer—opportunities that are often assumed to be absent from digitally mediated forms (Schaberg 2018). Teachers may refer to the importance of informal conversations with students in corridors and coffee shops and emphasize that co-presence within the classroom provides them with minute-by-minute feedback on the success or otherwise of their teaching through the immediacy of body language and eye contact. They may add that by making themselves available at the end of class, teachers enable responsive and individual communication with students and that by keeping regular office hours, they allow students to predict when their doors will be open for contact and consultation.

These are indeed all instances of the social and intellectual interactions with students that teachers enjoy. But in chapter 16 we argue that they are not inevitable and essential to what it means to do good teaching. Rather, they are enactments of the underlying academic values of accessibility, approachability, flexibility, and sensitivity to the personal and individual needs of students. Different teachers, depending on personality, experience, and material circumstances, enact these values in different ways. Here, we argue that what is important is not how they are enacted but that they are enacted. In exactly the same way that the sociomaterialities of the classroom and corridor provide campus-based teachers with opportunities to engage and interact with their students, the virtual spaces and places of the online mode provide ways for digitally mediated interactions between students and teachers to occur. There need be no stark divide. **Contact works in multiple ways. Face time is overvalued**. We also argue against the idea of the "online version," suggesting that by understanding online courses as versions of those delivered face-to-face, we limit them often—without necessarily intending to—assigning them to the second-best position. Online education needs its own "born digital" teaching methods that complement the pedagogies of co-presence, without trying to replicate them. **Digital education reshapes its subjects. The possibility of the "online version" is overstated.**

We then move on to argue in chapter 17 for a more nuanced understanding of what makes "place" in digital education. We suggest that the built spaces of the campus—traditionally seen and understood as the place where authentic higher education happens—need to be viewed through a more varied and nuanced description of what makes a place of learning. We use aspects of mobilities theory (Urry 2007) to challenge the ways in which we have traditionally aligned authentic education with physical co-presence in a built space. We argue instead for seeing the university as a place that is produced in multiple ways by the activities of its users, online and off—a space of flux and flow rather than a stable, bounded institution. New conceptualizations of presence are required in such a space, by which teachers and learners can build a new, shared imaginary of contact. **Place is differently, not less, important online.**

Finally, in chapter 18, we turn to distance education in particular, suggesting that we need to rethink what we mean when we talk about distance. Rather than emphasizing only the physical separation of objects or people in space, we foreground other, often more important, dimensions of communicative, temporal, and affective distance and their effects. In doing so, we move beyond a focus on distance education as a form of geospatial distancing that can be smoothed over by communications technology. Instead, we emphasize the potential challenges and opportunities that emerge when we work with the differences and distances that come with teaching online—time zones, political differences, cultural disjuncts—and argue that these are equally, if not more, important in building critical ways to do online teaching. **Distance is temporal, affective, political: not simply spatial.**

15

ONLINE CAN BE THE PRIVILEGED MODE. DISTANCE IS A POSITIVE PRINCIPLE, NOT A DEFICIT.

The still-common assumption that online learning is a lower-quality alternative to conventional campus-based approaches has historical and political roots. The roots are historical in the sense that early online course design emerged from correspondence course models of distance learning (Moore 2013), in which dialogue and scholarly community were replaced by individualized, often isolated self-study. Politically, as discussed in part I of this book, online innovation is frequently directed—or seen to be so—by the industrializing imperatives of economy and efficiency rather than by the desire to develop new forms of critical, engaged practice. These tensions still exist, amplified by the alignment (perceived but also, in many instances, real) of isolating, low-quality online education with extractive, for-profit models of higher education (McMillan Cottom 2017). Such assumptions support the belief that only face-to-face teaching and learning can be authentic, with the power of eye contact frequently cited as emblematic of the quality mark of face-to-face interaction.

Here, we offer alternative readings of how online teaching can enable learning that is not only connected and "real" but also, depending on pedagogical approach, has the potential to be of higher quality than some face-to-face modes. To begin, however, it is important to return to our assumptions about what technology is and therefore what it may do to online teaching and learning. As already outlined in part I and elsewhere, the approach to understanding online education informed by science and technology studies proposed by Hamilton and Friesen (2013) emphasizes the tendency to see technology in either instrumentalist or essentialist terms— either as a neutral tool that functions purely as an instrument of human intention or as an unstoppable force that drives and determines social change. Both instrumentalism and essentialism fail to take account of the social and material codependence of technology and its uses, black-boxing technology and closing it off from further examination (Bayne 2015).

To address this issue, we argue here, as elsewhere, for a sociomaterial perspective that acknowledges the social as inextricably entangled with the contextual and the material, understanding these as "continuously acting on each other to bring forth objects and knowledge" (Fenwick 2010, 105). Here, knowledge is not a prepackaged thing to be transmitted from one mind to another, unchanged by the medium of its transmission, but rather emerges from mutually constitutive sociomaterial relations. Such a perspective opens a space for us to shift away from an assumption that online is the lesser mode and understand it as something different, actively produced by its teachers and learners and determined by its contexts.

To build the case for distance as a positive principle, we start by attempting to counter two linked arguments often used

against the online mode: that embodied co-presence and proximity are a necessary underpinning for quality education and
that distance education is necessarily isolating, demotivating,
and therefore of lesser quality. Philosophies and psychologies
of human behavior that seek to separate mind from body are
centuries old and have long been challenged, yet were still
highly formative in the early days of the internet in general
(Barlow 1996), and online education in particular. One of the
most-read early texts (Dreyfus 2001, 47), built an entire argument around the idea that to be online was to become "dis-
embodied." Dreyfus argued that "only emotional, involved,
embodied human beings can become proficient and expert,"
rendering online education incapable of supporting advanced
study. Yet theory, from Stone's (1991) "Will the real body
please stand up?" to more current work on the constitutive
impact of the virtual on the materialization of identity in all
spaces, digital and physical (van Doorn 2011), has challenged
the view that to be online is to be somehow free of body.

When we feel elation or sadness as a result of the content
of an email or social media post, for example, we feel those
emotions in our bodies. The online learner is not protected
or isolated from the embodied excitements, triumphs, and
embarrassments of academic cut-and-thrust. If being online in
the late twentieth century offered the illusion of freedom from
body in the largely text-based digital environments we used
then, being online in the twenty-first makes us much more
visible to each other, more publicly engaged, often more vulnerable. Technology is no longer distancing; rather, it is its
proximities that have become problematic. Ubiquitous social
media demand display and the public crafting of self; platforms
extract personal data to bring advertisers intimate knowledge

of their users; creeping surveillance on campus eases us into a new normal of visibility. We discuss some of these issues further in part V.

At the same time, it might be argued that anyone who sits more than three rows back in a 500-seat lecture hall is a "distance learner." While students understand the potential of the live lecture for direct contact with their teachers, in many cases the experience is more parasocial—a one-sided relationship with only an illusion of reciprocity. We appreciate speakers who make eye contact with their audience, but we do not expect this to be meaningfully one-to-one. Massified higher education cannot, in many instances, be experienced as intimate. The idea that embodied proximity is essential to quality education is an outdated trope based in historical and elite models of university education in which students were inducted into scholarship by sitting at the feet of the master.

We are not arguing here that digitally mediated teaching is no different from face-to-face but rather that because it *is* different—and because our assumptions about teaching are often challenged when we take it online—it has the potential to be better in some contexts. Online learning, as we know, can be the basis for opening up a more inclusive form of education to students who need to be able to study without the constraints of being on-campus (working students, parents, disabled students), as well as opening university-level study to new, richly diverse global cohorts. Digital education puts teachers and students in a volatile, creative, and highly generative space where good teachers find their practice being opened up to new ways of doing things. Online film festivals, collectively written multimodal assignments, virtual walking tours, shared virtual fieldwork, and dynamic, ambient social media feeds are some examples from our own practice, and there are many others.

Other advantages of being online relate to the idea of risk taking as an important aspect of some kinds of learning. For example, it has been frequently observed that the online environment can facilitate participation in debate by the less confident, vocal, or verbally fluent of our students and that this can be attributed to the modest reduction of social cues present in that context (Hammick and Lee 2014). Less eye contact can be a release from some of the inhibitions that might be experienced in the classroom setting, allowing a skilled teacher to enable a level of manageable risk that works in favor of less confident students.

There are of course negative issues with the distance mode that need to be addressed. Distance can be privileged, but it is also true that learning online, particularly in its early days, was often reported as isolating and limited in terms of social contact, a factor often seen to relate to reduced motivation and high levels of dropout from online distance courses (Bekele 2010; Simpson 2013). Some more recent work continues to find a negative relationship between online learning and collaborative and social learning (Dumford and Miller 2018). The deficit model of online education often assumes a particular pedagogy in which repositories of self-paced, didactic materials are worked through in isolation and tested via multiple-choice assessments. The high profile of MOOCs has not been helpful in this regard, in that these have for the most part reinforced the alignment of digital education with teacher-light methods. Often touted as flexible anywhere-anytime learning, the self-paced model is often a mechanistic, anonymized learning experience that is not responsive to individual students' interests, skill levels, or needs. We heartily agree that this offers a lesser learning experience, likely to be demotivating and to lead to high levels of attrition. Other forms of online teaching—fully engaged, properly supported, creative, and community focused—are an entirely different matter.

Even within courses adopting these more engaged approaches, however, we have found evidence of what we call "campus envy" (Bayne, Knox, and Ross 2015). Campus envy is the tendency for some students, even those who are extremely happy with their online courses, to have the vague sense that their learning experience would somehow be even better if they were on campus. The feeling is often undefined and vague but is real for some, who see the idealized campus as a kind of touchstone—a guarantor of the authenticity of academic experience. We discuss the research underpinning the idea of campus envy in chapter 17. Further critical issues are raised in relation to the (often opaque) algorithms that structure our entry points to the social environments that digital educators commonly use (see part III). The threat that algorithmically driven targeting of political messages poses to contemporary democracy, for example, serves to fuel further the anxiety surrounding technologically mediated communications for education (Hindman 2018; Vaidhyanathan 2018).

All of these are reasons for maintaining a constantly critical stance toward the potential of online teaching and learning, and toward our own practice. Online teachers need to be ready to confront at individual, institutional, and political levels the tensions and challenges that emerge in these spaces. However, we should do this from a position of confidence in the quality and creativity of what we are able to offer online, not from a position that assumes "distance" or "online" carries an automatic deficit.

While poorly designed online courses may create isolating, demotivating experiences for students, collaborative, community-driven courses that may include opportunities for peer working and responsive and tailored tutor interaction and feedback are also possible; see, for instance, our own experiences of creating online dissertation festivals (O'Shea and Dozier 2014), collaborative assessments (O'Shea and Fawns 2014), playful experiments with automated teacherbots (Bayne 2015b), and participative learning analytics (Knox 2017b). There will of course be differences in the experience of being a student online, offline, or in a combined blended environment. While in our manifesto we argue that the online can be the privileged mode, we do not do so blindly. It is not always best, but it can—depending on context and design—be better. **Online can be the privileged mode. Distance is a positive principle, not a deficit.**

16

CONTACT WORKS IN MULTIPLE WAYS. FACE TIME IS OVERVALUED; DIGITAL EDUCATION RESHAPES ITS SUBJECTS. THE POSSIBILITY OF THE "ONLINE VERSION" IS OVERSTATED.

Here we continue the argument by bringing together two points from the manifesto that aim to resist seeing online teaching as a deficit mode. We begin by challenging the idea of contact as an organizing principle for higher education teaching that is applied to online contexts: **Contact works in multiple ways. Face time is overvalued**. We then argue against the—now largely historical—tendency to see online courses as versions of "proper courses taught face-to-face and on-campus: **Digital education reshapes its subjects. The possibility of the "online version" is overstated**.

First, what is "contact" in teaching, and why is it considered important? Engagement and responsive interaction between a student and a teacher are essential components of high-quality teaching in whatever mode (Bekele 2010), yet there remains a commonplace sense that these are achievable only through co-present interaction, with eye-to-eye contact often seen as the marker of authentic teaching. Colleges routinely use hours of contact—often understood in the traditional forms of the co-located lecture or seminar—as the primary spatial-temporal organizing device of the academic year.

In our manifesto, we challenge this organizing idea of contact as something that requires physical co-presence, arguing instead for a broader, richer understanding that does not assume face time as a default. We argue that contact can be seen as a sense of nearness and connection to others, a communicative moment that will necessarily be differently experienced in every coming together of people, technologies, and contexts. We suggest that "contact" in its educational sense needs to be rethought and shifted away from its implicit alignment with co-location, co-presence, and synchronicity, to be understood instead as a form of sociomaterial presence that can be enacted in many different ways, including online. It is in extended sociomaterial assemblages that students and teachers meet and make—or produce—contact. No communicative act is about unfettered transmission; all are produced through the social and material entanglements in which they are embedded.

Presence—and contact—are perhaps felt when it seems like nothing is getting in the way of apparently direct communicative interaction and a strived-for meeting of minds—that "perceptual illusion of non-mediation" referred to in the early years of the internet by Lombard and Ditton (1997, 29). Unmediated presence is, however, illusory across all communication modes. The face-to-face encounter is mediated by language, the spoken word, subtle expressions of the body; the literary encounter by the written word and the material properties of the book (typeface, paper, quality of print); and the online encounter by the configuration of screen, keyboard, device, and code. The sense of presence here lies in the perception of the absence of something that exists (language, print, screen). Digital environments in their complexity and frequent changes in form often foreground and confront us with the presence of mediation in a way that other media and moments do not. When the technology runs smoothly, the communicative mediation is elided, and only the intersubjective experience is felt.

Snapshot

In interrogating the pursuit of smoothness in communication, the artist Beverley Hood has explored the concept of the glitch. Hood (2012) describes a commission in which she employed professional dancers to choreograph the "disruptions, imperfections and glitches" experienced within digital games. Where programming errors, bandwidth issues, or lack of gamer expertise causes awkwardness and instability of play, Hood argues that an opportunity is opened up to think anew about the apparent perfection and smoothness of the digital environment.

Hood's project used dancers to choreograph and restage these glitches, looking at how real bodies cope with "the limits of such foreign and unnatural movement and subsequently, how this physically re-enacted choreography can be embedded and re-imaged within a responsive digital environment" (1). Using a Microsoft Kinect and large-screen display, the audience of Hood's work is asked to step into the digital shoes of a lead dancer character and attempt to follow the "intricate, glitch choreography performed by the dancing troupe on screen."

For us, this example of working with (rather than against) the disjunctures and imperfections of technology offers a way to better understand what it means to communicate and teach online.

> Hood's creative use of the point at which technological smoothness breaks down prompts us, as digital educators, to think about the apparently seamless mediation of co-present teaching, how that is troubled when we teach online, and what that means for the way we use glitches as teachers.

As many of our digital technologies have become smoother, more immersive, and less obtrusive, we find ourselves in a postdigital era in which we need to understand contact as something that takes place multiply: a video call is contact, and so is teacher presence on a Twitter feed; a phone call is contact, and so is a shared gaming session; an asynchronous text chat is contact, and so is a coauthoring session on a shared document. These are forms that we can value on their own terms, without always needing to align them with ideals of contact dependent on proximity in space, and visibility of face. **Contact works in multiple ways. Face time is overvalued.**

We can extend these ideas into the notion of versioning and the perceived authenticity, or otherwise, of online courses. When colleges and universities began to adopt online and distance education, the starting point for designing online courses was often an established course with the same name or curriculum that ran face-to-face. This approach was perhaps comforting: if the online version could be as close as possible to one that had already been established and run on-campus, then teachers and institutions would surely be on safe ground and the risks perceived as embedded in the new medium mitigated. The essential quality of a course, it might be argued, has the best chance of remaining intact within a new medium if it can align itself clearly to the more established and understood mode of delivery. If the quality and form of the on-campus course can be replicated online, then the authenticity and reliability of the online version can be assumed. In the second manifesto point considered here, we aim to challenge this view. **Digital education reshapes its subjects. The possibility of the "online version" is overstated.**

The focus on versioning implies that online is a deviation from the real thing, that the real course must be the one where humans are co-present in a physical environment. The assumption follows that if we cannot manage co-presence in our contemporary busy lives, then technology can come to the rescue as long as any associated deficits are remediated as much as possible. The focus of course design then becomes to closely replicate the trusted forms and methods of face-to-face teaching rather than to revel in the new and multiple creative pedagogies enabled by the digital environment.

Institutional support for online course design is often framed as mitigating the essential deficit of the online mode. For example, a set of quality review questions for new online courses issued by the University of California, Santa Barbara asks how these will "substitute for face-to-face lectures or meetings" and how verification of student identity will be achieved (University of California Santa Barbara, n.d.). In many ways it is right that such questions are asked, as they encourage course designers to think about the consequences of their decisions. However, it is a helpful thought exercise to consider how we might reverse the online/on-campus binary to privilege the former rather than the latter. For example, why, when setting quality standards for face-to-face courses, do we not ask: How would this course substitute for the lack of opportunities for self-pacing and asynchronous engagement achievable online? How would you ensure that the students have adequate multimodal experiences of their subject, such as those that are available online? How will you know your students have written their own assignments without regular text-based interactions such as blog and forum contributions that allow you to get to know their work and style of writing?

None of the above is intended to deny genuine concerns about the quality of online teaching and learning in some contexts, or its acknowledged challenges. Our argument here is that it is time to move away from seeing online, distance teaching as the deficit model and on-campus, face-to-face teaching as the touchstone of quality and authenticity. The online mode changes how we teach and how we understand ourselves as teachers and students. Teaching online reshapes its subjects in all senses of the word; we now need to move confidently beyond the idea of the version. **Digital education reshapes its subjects. The possibility of the "online version" is overstated**.

17

PLACE IS DIFFERENTLY, NOT LESS, IMPORTANT ONLINE.

What is the place of "place" in online, distance education? And what does it mean to be "at" college when students are not physically "on" the campus? Here, we suggest that we need to develop ways of thinking about place that shift us away from the default privileging of physical presence on campus and understand distance and online students as positioned in multiple ways to academic institutions, simultaneously inside and outside them, here and not here, at the same time both present and absent in ways that are pedagogically productive.

The term *distance education* is itself a negative definition. "Distance" education is distant *from* something; it is what is not located on-campus; it is described and often downgraded, seen as other to the norm. The terminology of distance in this way constructs an apparently clear relation between absence and presence that needs to be challenged. Our own research (for example, Bayne, Gallagher, and Lamb, 2014) has shown subtleties in the ways that distance students understand institutional space and place that need to be accounted for when we do distance and online teaching. While students highly value the networks and flow of the digital environments we use, the material campus continues to be symbolically and materially significant to them, despite that fact that they may never physically attend that campus or even wish to. We have also found that the ways in which some distance students imagine and privilege the idea of the campus can lead them to misattribute difficulties common across all modes of study (such as difficult relationships and time pressures) specifically to the online mode (Ross and Sheail 2017).

We have found mobilities theory to be particularly useful for building a better understanding of this complex orientation to place among distance students. Urry (2007) describes the mobilities paradigm as a shift that "enables the 'social world' to be theorized as a wide array of . . . practices, infrastructures and ideologies that all involve, entail or curtail various kinds of movement of people, or ideas, or information or objects" (6). Mobilities theory "puts into question the fundamental 'territorial' and 'sedentary' precepts of twentieth-century social science" (Hannam, Sheller, and Urry 2006, 2). It is centrally concerned with distance and the ways in which this is articulated, negotiated, and traversed.

The idea of sedentarism, outlined by Sheller and Urry (2006), is particularly useful in examining the "place" of digital and distance education. Sedentarism "treats as normal stability, meaning, and place, and treats as abnormal distance, change, and placelessness" (208). It sees "bounded and authentic places or regions or nations as the fundamental basis of human identity and experience" and takes "territorial nationalism" as its guiding principle (209). If we apply this thinking to distance and online education, we can see this sedentarist privileging of the bounded space of the built campus being played out in various ways, from the way the language of distance negatively defines what we do when we teach online, to the dependence on outmoded definitions of contact we addressed above, to the reliance on institutional promotional materials on alluring images of university estates and buildings. This final factor plays a key part in anchoring institutional authenticity—and access to high levels of academic capital—to the image of the built estate, in the process fetishizing the campus and the enclosed bricks and mortar spaces of the university. It is partly through this fetishization of the campus that the university has been able to create its "insiders" and its "outsiders" in a dependence on the idea of the university as a built space that bounds and constitutes its authenticity.

Thinking about distance education from a mobilities perspective helps us to interrogate these sedentarist assumptions in favor of a more nuanced way of understanding the many, complex ways in which both distance students and increasingly mobile cohorts of on-campus students describe and make the space of the university. The university, we suggest, can no longer be seen as a bounded, stable entity—a static container within which education takes place. Instead it is recast as a complex enactment (Edwards, Tracy, and Jordan 2011, 22) by which "hosts, guests, buildings, objects, and machines are contingently brought together to produce certain performances in certain places at certain times" (Sheller and Urry 2006, 214). In doing digital education, we move beyond the spatial securities (Mol and Law 1994) of the campus, toward an understanding of the institution as characterized by "flux and flows rather than simple bounded space" (Fenwick, Edwards, and Sawchuk 2011, 153).

Our research found a strong symbolic and sentimental connection for some of our distance students with the city and campuses of the University of Edinburgh, though this did not necessarily equate to straightforward sedentarism. Heritage, diaspora, and home were very real factors influencing distance students located often at very great distances from the built university. One US-based student who had traced his family back to two migrations from Scotland to Massachusetts described his attendance at an online Edinburgh program as "very much my own virtual 'Homecoming Scotland'" (see Bayne et al. 2014).

While these new kinds of "homing" are made possible by digital technologies, the space of the university is also produced in new ways by these highly mobile cohorts of students who make their classrooms in hotel rooms, offices, cafés, airports and bus stations, always with a bringing together of multiple devices, internet connections, texts, teachers, and peers (Sheail 2018). Our research has found that the place and site of learning, and of the university itself, was for these students continually being reenacted as they moved between different elements of their program (different courses or modules), between different learning environments (teaching takes place across multiple formal, social, open, closed, visual, textual, synchronous, and asynchronous digital environments on our digital education program), between different course communities, between multiple means of access (laptop, desktop, smartphone, tablet) and equally across many regional and national boundaries. What it means to be "on the course" or to be "at" college is never one thing; it is always multiple, enacted differently for every student almost at every moment. A sense of home, of place, is important for these students, but it is one that is made, performed and enacted in ways that open up new understandings of what we mean by "campus." **Place is differently, not less, important online.**

18

DISTANCE IS TEMPORAL, AFFECTIVE, POLITICAL: NOT SIMPLY SPATIAL.

Here we continue our discussion of the ways in which the distance between people, materials, and objects is often surfaced as the primary (spatial) challenge for digital education. However, we move on to considering other aspects of educational contexts that should be taken into account, particularly in relation to the diverse experiences of students.

Partly due to a narrow conceptualization of contact, emphasis has often been placed on closely replicating through technology the experience of face-to-face teaching in order to mitigate or minimize students' sense of being spatially distanced. Communication through digital technologies and environments of course offers opportunities for connecting students and teachers over great physical distances. However, we argue here that potential smoothness in the appearance or operation of a digital environment should not disguise or obscure the temporal, affective, and political distances, differences, and disjuncts that give context to an online educational experience. The technological smoothing over of spatial distance needs to be accompanied by a pedagogy that recognizes and meaningfully incorporates complexity and diversity.

Our proposition is that in discussions about how to do digital education, we need to engage more critically with its temporal, affective, and political dimensions. These aspects of an education may be invisible—below the digital surface—but they are also essential to ways of working with students to build a better understanding of the context of a course of study. In drawing out aspects of temporality, affect, and the political in education spaces, it is not our intention to suggest that we can consider time without space or politics without affect (see Massumi 2015), but rather to begin exploring more complex ways of thinking about the educational experience through relevant strands of the literature in these areas.

Massey's (2005) discussion of the "event of place" is helpful in considering digital education as a particular kind of "throwntogetherness": of times, places, bodies, voices, images, texts, sounds, and technologies that present various opportunities for exploration and understanding in the context of a course. The idea of "negotiating a here-and-now . . . drawing on a history and a geography of thens and theres" (140) seems highly appropriate to working with a globally distributed group of students, teachers, and technologies, all bringing their own geographies and histories—both personal (a unique set of experiences) and local (a current context)—to a course of study.

In the time studies literature, for example, in work on standardized time, biological time, and globalization, Birth (2012) highlights the flattening potential of information technology that operates on clock time. He expands on the way in which work to standardize time can have the significant effect of obscuring the various rhythms of biological time, such as those relating to daylight and the human body. For Birth, modern capitalism "treat[s] the Earth as if it is flat . . . connecting people and places in ways that negate distance" (122) and neglecting the complexity of "globeness" (Birth 2012). Our own research (Sheail 2018) has suggested that universities should no longer view distance and digital education as a form of reaching out to the wider world beyond the campus, but must instead understand education in terms of globeness, as an *"opening up* of the idea of the university; embodied and imagined through strong connections across multiple locations, times and temporalities" (Sheail 2018, 56). We need to understand digital education as occupying its own particular, multiply layered and shifting time-space—one that needs to be addressed on its own terms rather than always in relation to that of the physical campus.

One example Sheail (2018) uses is that of an online program with a highly international cohort spread across multiple time zones. One student is based in a country going through a period of political unrest during which a curfew has been put in place, alongside a power shutdown, after 10:00 p.m. Because of this, the teacher and other students in the cohort have worked to reorganize their synchronous online seminars to be outside the hours of curfew. As Sheail argues, this example is important

> because it isn't just about finding a convenient time in relation to a time zone, but relates the correspondence of the student time-space to a national, geopolitical time-space (a state of emergency), and back to the time-space of the University . . . some four thousand physical miles away. (64–65)

The example emphasizes how the temporality of teaching online is as much about the experienced time of individual students, about globeness and the times we live in, as it is about the campus's clock time. Teaching within such a temporal reconfiguration requires teachers and institutions to acknowledge the complexity of these. Rather than seeing time zones and temporal disjunctures as problems to be solved, we should see them as a positive opportunity to develop our pedagogy by taking proper account of the diversity of experience to be found in our student cohorts.

Implicated in globeness are, of course, the forces of affect. Wetherell (2012) draws attention to the different disciplinary approaches to affect from researchers who have a particular interest in studying emotion to those with a broader interest in affect in relation to the influence of forces and change, where affect is not specific to human experience: "the sun affects the moon, a magnet affects iron filings, and the movement of waves affects the shape of the coastline" (2). In the education literature, however, affect is more often more narrowly considered in terms of emotion. In exploring the affective domain, Quinlan (2016), for example, identifies four important relationships in higher education that have potential for emotional engagement: from the student-staff relationship with an academic subject, to relationships between students and their teachers, to relationships with peers, and the relationship with a developing self.

To broaden our understanding of affect away from individual emotion and its measurement and shift reductive ideas about globalization and global access to something more oriented to globeness, we need to develop speculative digital methods for making affective connections. One example of this—from design research rather than education—that we have found inspiring is the earthquake shelf, developed by interaction designers Selby and Kirk (2015).

Snapshot

Interaction designers Selby and Kirk (2015) developed an earthquake shelf design experiment: a shelf furniture installation that looks much like an ordinary wall-mounted bookshelf that is linked to a live data feed of earthquake activity. When an earthquake occurs somewhere in the world, the earthquake shelf shakes, and objects that have been placed on it may be disturbed or broken. In this way, the force of an earthquake event happening at a distance can create material and affective consequences for those in physical proximity to the location of the shelf.

Working with a research participant who had previously experienced the local effects of earthquake activity, the researcher-designers noted three phases of participant response to the activity of the shelf when located in the participant's office, "from an emotional connection to [the participant's previous] experience, to an empathetic connection to others, before the shelf's effects finally 'wore off'" (10). While the project was initially developed as a design experiment related to memory, the shelf design became a live indicator of potentially devastating seismic activity.

This design project brings critical moments in other places to attention, either to an immediate audience or by leaving a material effect—damaged or displaced items from the shelf display—to be discovered later. It creates a sensory experience underpinned by the idea of an event in one place generating an effect in another. The earthquake shelf brings its audience closer materially but also temporally to those experiencing the earthquake effect locally. Although the immediate risk to the shelf audience from the earthquake is reduced almost to nothing, the shelf draws attention to the connectedness of events in the world.

To apply this thinking specifically to a context of online education, we briefly describe an activity incorporated into one of the courses in the digital education master's program that we teach. A recent cohort of thirty-one students taking our course An Introduction to Digital Environments for Learning (IDEL) connected students in physical locations in Canada, England, Germany, Haiti, India, the Netherlands, Pakistan, Scotland, Spain, Sudan, Switzerland, and the United Arab Emirates. Multiple locations mean that consideration needs to be given to multiple time zones, but at the same time, and in direct relation to the course, multiple education systems and technological infrastructures, including restricted access to some modes of delivery (for example, sufficient bandwidth to support video streaming) and platforms (government blocking of certain areas of the internet, for example).

These contexts and conditions for education are also unquestionably political. In this kind of internationally distributed but connected group of students and teachers, numerous political and powerful structures inevitably influence educational and professional contexts as well as the technologies engaged. In ways that can be simultaneously positive and problematic, digital environments have the potential to disguise these influences, smoothing them over and surfacing only common interests and directed discussions. It is equally possible, however, that the political context comes into view. Political and economic structures overlap with technological infrastructures, with effects on access to electricity, hardware, and media. It is not unusual in the context of a global online course for students to become caught up, directly or indirectly, in major political events that may affect digital, physical, and psychological space and safety. Even experienced at a distance, events reported in the international mainstream media may have local effects that are distressing or distracting.

One of the recommended activities for the IDEL course is for students to visualize and share with the group a digital postcard or other representation that communicates their experience of participating in the course and their relationships with the various digital environments explored. (At the time of writing, these might include the current learning platform, Moodle, and the course spaces we connect to from it, such as *Minecraft*, Twitter, other social media, and various audio and videoconferencing applications.) At this point in the course (usually around the midpoint in a semester), students have established familiar routines, processes, and locations for particular kinds of interactions with course materials, staff, and each other. Whether through the use of image, audio, or video, digital collages of student spaces and places emerge. Through this activity, moving commuter spaces, workplaces, and outdoor vistas begin to surface, connecting the cohort to the diversity of other student experiences—both digital and physical—on the course. These visual (sometimes interactive) representations of places and practices, connected through the day-to-day experiences of students, merge to form complex accounts of their learning environments. In recent instances of the course, examples have ranged from an interactive Google Earth mapping of the entire networked cohort, to a head-cam videoed and narrated cycle commute, exploring the study space between home and work.

Snapshot

The Elektronisches Lernen Muzik project is an ongoing learning playlist project, set up for our students as a way of exploring "the role that music plays in influencing, informing and inspiring learning activity" (Lamb, n.d.). Digital education students and staff, situated in multiple locations but connected by their participation in a program of study, are encouraged to contribute playlists, curated either individually or by a course group, to be uploaded to a dedicated project website. Playlist curators are invited to include sleeve notes, track listings, introductory notes, and images or artwork and are asked to comment on the relationship of the track to the learning environment, study activity, or other aspect of a course.

Playlist 22, for example, is curated by a group of second-year architecture students, bringing together the tracks that keep them going through long nights in the studio. This is a high-energy playlist. One of the students points out when nominating the song "Time" (by Jungle) in the design studio, "You can't jump around so I divert the energy into my mind. It helps me get into a rhythm."

The sharing of curated playlists is a sharing of elements of individuals' learning environments and practices, but it is also a curation and analysis of affective responses stimulated by or reflected in music. It allows participants to share connective experiences that go beyond the discussion and analysis of curriculum content to explore particular academic practices, such as reading, writing, searching, making, editing, and the environmental adjustments needed to support these. The playlist site also has its own temporal relationship to the program of study and its participants. Playlists remain as students graduate and as new students begin their studies. As the site is open and public, the playlists remain available for repeated play with a life beyond the duration of their curators' studies. The site is one of many digital environments in the life of an online course that becomes a place where affective traces are left.

Our key proposition for practice, explored in the brief examples given here, is that there are many creative opportunities for exploring digital connections that move beyond the digital reproduction of the face-to-face encounter (such as the videoconference or lecture). These are methods that can be developed and adapted to acknowledge and work with the local temporalities and specificities of a highly diverse group of students, acknowledging global differences and disjuncts in a way that disturbs the smoothing, flattening effects of some digital environments, especially those designed to emulate a particular kind of classroom space with its associated hierarchies. The design of digital education offers new opportunities for exploring a global network that not only allows for the development of deeper and more creative connections among students but also has the capacity to increase our critical understanding of localized and environmental conditions, professions, policies, and practices. At the same time, it offers us as teachers a way to become more attuned to the experience of distance students and their relationships to an educational environment that is simultaneously time temporal, affective, and political. It allows us to glimpse globeness in all its technological and political complexity. **Distance is temporal, affective, political: not simply spatial.**

CONCLUSION: BEYOND THE DEFICIT MODEL

In this part, we have argued against the common perspective that online education is in essence an inferior mode, by exploring and countering some of the claims made against it.

Online can be the privileged mode. Distance is a positive principle, not a deficit.

Contact works in multiple ways. Face time is overvalued.

Digital education reshapes its subjects. The possibility of the "online version" is overstated.

Place is differently, not less, important online.

Distance is temporal, affective, political: not simply spatial

We have argued that online can be a privileged mode, suggesting that many of the negative discourses surrounding it can be traced back to a historical tendency to see it in relation to education conducted face-to-face. To begin to value digital and online education and develop a more sophisticated critique, we need to consider it in context and on its own terms, understanding digital education as neither a single model of efficient delivery nor simply an interruption of conventional, co-present teaching. In our view, it is better seen as a shifting configuration of place within which new kinds of teaching practice can emerge.

The chapters in this part discussed some key terms indicative of how digital practice has been constrained by its conventional, on-campus referents: how "contact" and "presence" have traditionally acted as markers for quality teaching, how online courses have often been seen merely as "versions" of "real" ones, how online teaching spaces have been seen as shadowy substitutes for the bricks and mortar of "real" campuses, and how the messy complexity of globally distributed student cohorts has been too readily smoothed over by the language of "anytime, anyplace learning" and its associated teaching methods.

We have made the—still sometimes contentious—argument that online teaching can be better than on-campus teaching. Creative, committed online practice can create deeper and richer learning experiences that are appropriate for a postdigital world. As teachers, we should see this as an opportunity to rethink and remake our educational practices—to consider not only what we have previously done but why we have done it and how it can be done better.

V

SURVEILLANCE AND
(DIS)TRUST

MANIFESTO POINTS COVERED

Online courses are prone to cultures of surveillance. Visibility
    is a pedagogical and ethical issue.
A routine of plagiarism detection structures-in distrust.

Figure 5.1

INTRODUCTION

The chapters in this part discuss two closely linked manifesto points that explore how teaching with technology requires us to attend to issues of surveillance, visibility, ethics, and trust. The relationship between surveillance and distrust is one that we explore throughout. Our argument is that practices of surveillance have the effect of reducing, rather than increasing, levels of trust between students, teachers, administrators, and technologists in higher education settings. For this reason, bringing these manifesto points together helps to shed light not only on the practices but the implications of surveillance technologies in higher education. These implications are felt even when the stated intention of the technology is something

Work on this part was written up and presented at the Networked Learning 2018 Conference, Zagreb, Croatia. Ross, J., and H. Macleod. 2018. "Surveillance, (Dis)trust and Teaching with Plagiarism Detection Technology." In *Proceedings of the 11th International Conference on Networked Learning 2018*, edited by M. Bajić, N. B. Dohn, M. de Laat, P. Jandrić, and T. Ryberg, 235–242. Zagreb: Zagreb University of Applied Sciences.

other than surveillance—for example, in plagiarism detection systems. It is the effects, not the intentions, that matter here.

In digital education practices, instrumental goals such as enhancement and efficiency, explored in different ways throughout this book, are often addressed through centralizing technology decisions that need to be understood in terms of visibility and surveillance. Drawing on Lyon's concept of a surveillance culture (2017), we examine how learning technologists, teachers, students, and college and university leaders participate in, respond to, resist, and rework their own and others' surveillance. We critique a commonly expressed assertion that surveillance technologies can be used benevolently (for example, by guiding students gently toward good academic practice or by helping teachers to identify struggling students). Instead, we suggest that these technologies act with and on already problematic conditions of digital visibility that are pervasive in the wider digital culture beyond the university and require critical and thoughtful responses from teachers within higher education institutions. **Online courses are prone to cultures of surveillance. Visibility is a pedagogical and ethical issue.**

We then move on to discuss how logics of surveillance are strongly at work in practices that attempt to regulate student behavior by subjecting bodies, as well as writing and other online activities, to algorithmic scanning and monitoring. These logics frame students as in need of careful monitoring to ensure that learning and teaching run smoothly. Routines of plagiarism detection, we argue, frame academic writing as a space in which dishonesty is rampant but preventable through technology, and by doing this, they intervene negatively in one of the most important sites of the student-teacher relationship:

the production and assessment of student work. We use the term *relationship* here in a moral and intersubjective sense. It is a relationship of collegiality, of reciprocal care and trust among teachers, students, academic managers, technologists, and leaders. Where these relationships become risk averse and mutually suspicious, trust is lost and not easily regained. We argue that plagiarism detection is a key—because routinized—site within which the effects of distrust are surfaced.

Directing digital education toward more positive futures than the ones mapped for us by surveillance and distrust requires finding ways to resensitize ourselves and our students to the values we want to shape our teaching. We need to better articulate what forms of privacy students have a right to expect from their educational experiences, offering means by which students can voice their responses to surveillance cultures in higher education. Such issues need to be addressed at a strategic level within our institutions and the sector more widely. In our reviews of technology platforms and practices, we argue for the need to move beyond issues of compliance and functional requirements, and toward more engagement with ethics and the nature and purpose of the university itself.

19

ONLINE COURSES ARE PRONE TO CULTURES OF SURVEILLANCE. VISIBILITY IS A PEDAGOGICAL AND ETHICAL ISSUE.

Higher education, like other sectors, is now intensely technologically mediated with most aspects of administration, research, and teaching suffused with digital process. Goals of quality, efficiency, and transparency lead to strategic and operational decisions being made about technology that are intensifying the datafication of academic productivity, engagement, and outputs. Activity is increasingly subject to normative processes of algorithmic exposure and measurement (Lorenz 2012), with academics becoming more and more entangled in what Lyon (2017) refers to as a "surveillance culture." Defining the term, Lyon describes it as "people actively participating in an attempt to regulate their own surveillance and the surveillance of others" (824). This participation need not be enthusiastic or strategic, but it indicates a different situation from the one Lyon and others previously described as surveillance society:

> Surveillance society is a concept originally used to indicate ways in which surveillance was spilling over the rims of its previous containers—government departments, policing agencies,

workplaces—to affect many aspects of daily life. But the emphasis was still on how surveillance was carried out by certain agencies in ways that increasingly touched the routines of social
life—from outside, as it were. This concept was often used in
ways that paid scant attention to citizens', consumers', travel-
ers', or employees' experience of and engagement with surveillance. (826)

A surveillance society framing, then, is one where surveillance is, by and large, understood as being done to people by
agencies. Surveillance culture, by contrast, is characterized by
attention to "widespread compliance with surveillance" (Lyon
2017, 828), and the way people "participate in, actively engage
with, and initiate surveillance themselves" (829). It is closely
linked to more benign concepts such as sharing, safety, and
transparency.

These concepts are far from neutral, however. Transparency,
for instance, as O'Neill (2002) puts it, "has marginalised the
more basic and important obligation not to deceive," replacing trust with accountability (Ellaway et al. 2015). Transparency in this view seeks to formalize away the moral imperative
not to deceive, seeking to remove the vulnerability that is the
essential element of a trusting, reciprocal relationship while
potentially masking a capacity to cheat. Similarly, sharing,
when cast as an imperative rather than a choice, removes from
individuals the agency that makes such an act meaningful and
obscures the motivations of those doing the sharing.

Natural desires for connection and security, in a technological and market-driven context that generates and thrives on
massive amounts of data, create practices that can be understood as "soft surveillance" (Lyon 2017, 833). A particularly
important feature of surveillance in its cultural sense is that
it is not necessarily or even primarily clandestine; it is better

understood as a set of relations or a sensibility and the values aligned with it (transparency, sharing, safety) as contingent and provisional. There are connections here to the critique of openness that we discussed in part III.

Lyon (2017) argues that questions around visibility are ethical ones and that "surveillance ought not merely to be *of* people . . . so much as *for* people—and thus should be practiced carefully and held to account" (835). In addition, as Zuboff (2015) argues, "human fallibility in the execution of contracts is the price of freedom" (81). Zuboff critiques claims that surveillance enables new contractual forms, describing it in terms of what she calls "Big Other," where "habitats inside and outside the human body are saturated with data and produce radically distributed opportunities for observation, interpretation, communication, influence, prediction, and ultimately modification of the totality of action." This is the "un-contract," in her terms, where the autonomy needed to enter into contracts gives way to the "rewards and punishments of a new kind of invisible hand" (82).

Those of us who work in digital education contexts are aware that many of the spaces in which we meet to engage in online education create data trails that make them at least potentially, if not currently, subject to practices of surveillance, analytics, and data mining, whether for educational or commercial purposes (or, often, both). Srnicek's (2017) work on platform capitalism highlights the mechanisms through which data are produced, extracted, monetized, stored, monitored, and reconfigured in a new model of value that relies on individual participation and interaction on platforms. Platform providers are agnostic about the kinds of interactions that produce these valuable data as long as the data keep flowing, and—as we saw in part III in the discussion of MOOC data—digital education settings can be a gold mine of these flows. These issues are becoming more pronounced as the consequences of digital data tracking and analysis become more significant and better understood. Movement through physical campus space, for example, leaves readable digital trails, as when students swipe an ID card to enter campus buildings. Where our manifesto says "online courses," we therefore take this to apply to all courses with significant technology elements, whether part of the teaching, the administration, or the assessment of the course.

Teacher-student relationships are changed by cultures of surveillance in the university, and technology is implicated in these cultures. Indeed, ways of understanding flows of power and agency in the contemporary university might usefully be mapped by exploring how surveillance cultures operate. To the extent that the human-technology teaching assemblage is constituted in ways often beyond the control of individual teachers, we need to consider collectively what kind of datafied future it is that we want and how we go about building this on a set of values that we can align to as professionals.

One area of intensification of visibility in the university is the implementation and continual upgrading of the technological tracking of student engagement. As we discussed in part III, the field of learning analytics has been at the forefront of this work in recent years, with extensive attention paid to the potential of analytics for improving assessment, feedback, prediction of student success, self-regulated learning, and more (Papamitsiou and Economides 2014). Less attention has been paid to the implications of such tracking on the intensification of surveillance cultures in higher education and on the expectations of students and teachers for how much student activity, work, and engagement should be monitored. As Prinsloo and Slade (2016) explain,

> Students often have no insight into the data collected by their HEI and so there is no possibility that data can be verified or any context provided. Considering the asymmetrical relationship of students and their institutions, students potentially then become quantified selves based on, for example, the number of log-ins, clicks, downloads, or time-on-task. (177)

For Prinsloo and Slade, recognition of the impacts of surveillance on configurations of vulnerability is a key factor in ensuring ethical and pedagogical appropriateness of learning analytics in higher education.

On the physical campus, attendance is often used as a proxy for engagement and student location data gathered for the purposes of attendance monitoring at lectures and seminars, as well as presence in other settings, for example libraries. Looking at a range of attendance policies from UK universities, for example, there is a common pattern in how they describe their purposes in monitoring attendance. They regularly refer to research that has found that attendance or participation correlates with higher grades for university students (see Lukkarinen, Koivukangas, and Seppälä 2016), implying a causal relationship, and they often describe attendance monitoring as aiming to support student achievement. They note that absences might indicate students who are struggling, and tracking attendance can be used to flag potential issues and follow up with students who may need help. Finally, they regularly cite government regulations for the monitoring of international students on particular kinds of visas. Macfarlane (2013) identifies a further work preparation argument for this monitoring (82).

In his later work on student freedom, Macfarlane (2016) categorizes attendance monitoring as one of a number of processes in the contemporary university that "demonstrate both a lack of trust in students and failure to respect their freedom to learn as an adult" (81). As a form of "bodily performativity," it stands in for learning that is not easy to measure and blurs the distinction between presence and engagement. As these systems become ever more intensive, there are seemingly never enough attendance data and they are never foolproof enough. The notion of the loophole (for example, the potential for a student to carry a classmate's ID card and swipe that person in) becomes a reason to develop ever more invasive methods, from manually signing in to ID card swiping, bluetooth/RFID scanning of devices, fingerprint scanning, and facial recognition.

Snapshot

In early 2018, staff members on an email list for those interested in technology and teaching at our university were asked by a colleague for ideas and advice about digital methods of attendance tracking. Practical solutions and technical ideas were exchanged, but as the thread evolved, a number of responses pointed out the problematic nature of treating this as simply a technical matter. A range of justifications for monitoring attendance was highlighted, including to satisfy international student visa requirements, fulfill a duty of care to students by knowing where they are, facilitate resource planning, and be able to intervene supportively if individual student attendance seems lacking. However, participants in the discussion expressed concern about the conflation of "attendance" and "engagement" ("I find it disappointing that at this point in time we still equate sitting in a particular place . . . with being 'engaged'"), and the dangers of ever more intensive data collection without clear benefits ("Don't rush to collect data you don't need, because data start leaking and not because of system failures. As soon as they know you have it, various busybodies will decide that they are entitled to a slice of it"). Furthermore, there was cynicism about the extent to which these practices were driven primarily by immigration regulations requiring universities to keep their international visa holders under surveillance, with other justifications as window dressing. The extent to which this is factually the case is perhaps less important than the sense of distrust of the various motivations behind attendance monitoring. Some staff see the politics of attendance monitoring as highly contestable.

The movement of students both on-campus and online is of increasing interest to researchers as they seek to determine which forms of movement and behavior correlate with academic success, and this interest is echoed in policies and practices that attempt to gather more, and more varied, data to analyze. The so-called intelligent campus (JISC 2017) has at its heart a focus on generating, analyzing, and interpreting data from the people who move within its virtual and physical boundaries. This may have value, although as Gašević, Dawson, and Siemens (2015) point out, researching what behaviors correlate with positive outcomes, and then mandating those behaviors, is ultimately likely to prove profoundly counterproductive, not least because of the nonequivalence of correlation and causation.

We suggest in our manifesto point that gathering extensive tracking data to see what is useful is not neutral. It has implications beyond the specific use, and it ushers in an orientation to students as sources of data that can be unproblematically mined and analyzed in the interests of

institutional performance and efficiency. As teachers, we
need to confront the negative ethical and pedagogic aspects
of creeping surveillance on campus and resist the uncritical
assumption that the intensification of monitoring and tracking of students is somehow inevitable. **Online courses are
prone to cultures of surveillance. Visibility is a pedagogical
and ethical issue.**

20

A ROUTINE OF PLAGIARISM DETECTION STRUCTURES-IN DISTRUST.

Finally, we explore one particularly pervasive form of monitoring of students in the university: automated plagiarism detection. At the time of writing (summer 2019), one of the largest of the software systems providing this service, Turnitin, had just been sold to the media conglomerate Advance Publications for the sum of US$1.5 billion. Commentators were quick to point out that this huge valuation rested in large part on the perceived value of Turnitin's data set (many millions of student assignments), highlighting the intellectual property concerns this raised (McKie 2019) and emphasizing the negative impact on trust implied by routinized use of such services. Here we take this matter of trust and examine it further, particularly in relation to the dangers of routine plagiarism detection for relationships of trust between students and teachers.

Philosopher Annette Baier (1986) defines *interpersonal trust* as "accepted vulnerability to another's possible but not expected ill will" (235). She explains that trust is necessary because "no one is able by herself to look after everything she wants to have looked after, nor even alone to look after her own 'private' goods, such as health and bodily safety" (1986, 236). Trust exists because of interpersonal risk and vulnerability: "where there is no vulnerability there is no need for trust" (Tschannen-Moran and Hoy 1998, 337). This vulnerability can extend in both directions in, for example, a teacher-student relationship. Townley and Parsell (2004) characterize this as a situation where "students risk error, failure, humiliation, teachers risk disappointment, deception, and indifference" (275). Power imbalances make trusting relationships more (and more complicated) than a simple contract between consenting people.

At an organizational level, trust makes possible the smooth operation of day-to-day business, minimizing costly and time-consuming practices of control and maintaining social relationships (McEvily, Perrone, and Zaheer 2003, 98). Lack of trust undermines the exercise of professional autonomy and agency by staff, risking that institutions could become paralyzed by more and more control practices. Yet leadership in higher education has been shifting toward regulation and away from trust (Olssen and Peters 2005, 324) in a managerialist turn that sees education activity as analogous to industrial production. As such, teaching is increasingly understood via concepts of regulation, efficiency, and economy (Hall 2016; Lynch 2006), aligned to the commodification of colleges and universities that we outlined in part I. In higher education settings, a culture of surveillance, facilitated and intensified by technology, risks creating conditions that are highly risk averse and destructive of the trust basis on which academic and student autonomy and agency rely. Technology architectures introduced to build trust by mapping performance may end up directly undermining these very goals (Tschannen-Moran and Hoy, 1998), as we exemplify here in the case of plagiarism detection systems.

Plagiarism detection software generally works as an intermediary layer between the student (who submits writing online either directly using the service or through a virtual learning environment which that connects to it) and the teacher (who retrieves the writing and provides feedback and a grade, often within the same online system). The plagiarism detection software applies matching algorithms to the submitted work, comparing it to the many hundreds of thousands of texts contained in its database. The higher the match, the higher the similarity score the work will receive. Teachers receive this score, along with color-coded views of the student's text, when they retrieve the work from the system. Plagiarism detection systems are of course just one example of the surveillance culture in which higher education now operates. However, it is a particularly striking one because of how widespread, accepted, and normalized it is (the Turnitin website claims "over 15,000 institutions in over 140 countries"; Turnitin, n.d.), and how explicitly it intervenes in one of the core tasks that students and their teachers conduct: the production and assessment of student work.

Plagiarism detection systems need to be seen not only in terms of how well they meet their stated aims (and there is some evidence that they do not do this particularly well; see Youmans 2011), but in terms of their other effects, such as on cultures of surveillance on the institution. Zwagerman (2008) argues that "plagiarism detection treats writing as a product, grounds the student-teacher relationship in mistrust, and requires students to actively comply with a system that marks them as untrustworthy" (692). He sees these systems as "the inevitable end point of the integrity scare: an efficient, perhaps even foolproof, technology of surveillance" (691). Morris and Stommel (2017) note that in addition, plagiarism detection platforms turn student intellectual property into profit for private companies, such as Turnitin, which are not accountable to them. Whatever teachers intend, however benevolent their individual purposes in deploying plagiarism detection software, we argue that their own practices, and indeed what it means to teach, are altered in the process, and not for the better.

Logics of surveillance are strongly at work in the practices of plagiarism detection, which attempt to regulate student behavior through the exposure of their writing to algorithmic scanning and monitoring. Such logics see dishonesty, cheating, and other negative behaviors as inevitable if not actively prevented, see students as needing careful monitoring, for their own good and for the smooth functioning of the learning and teaching process, and finally understand dishonesty as having the potential to be screened out through the use of technology.

Much of the critical literature around plagiarism detection practices explores, in one form or another, the shifting, historically specific, and thorny terrain of authorship (Blair 2011; Marsh 2004; Vie 2013), an issue that has been highlighted by networked writing practices including collaboration and remix. We explored this territory in part II of this book, in which we described the ways in which digital writing reworks traditional conceptions of authorship. Plagiarism detection processes oversimplify these complex issues and trajectories, implying a clear-cut answer to conceptually very difficult questions around what is meant by originality.

Plagiarism detection systems are claimed to act as both a deterrent and a method of identification of work that may be plagiarized (plagiarism detection companies are generally careful to stress that the decision about what constitutes plagiarism is always one for the human teacher to make). Many claims are made about the effectiveness of these systems in helping students learn about good academic practice (Mphahlele and McKenna 2019), particularly where students are allowed to run their work through the system before formally submitting assignments. They are also claimed to save time for teachers and—in what is a familiar theme extending through this book—to cast teachers as being deficient by being more effective at identifying plagiarism than the teacher alone can be. They offer to make visible what might otherwise be hidden or missed. This visibility is at the heart of the surveillance culture operating in colleges and universities and the changed relationships it builds between students and teachers.

Fundamentally, being monitored cannot be perceived as a neutral act, and the implication that good behavior is not anticipated signals that the one doing the checking assumes a relationship of distrust, which breeds distrust in return. In addition, the language around plagiarism frames it ideologically as a moral or cultural failing on the part of individual students (for example, through the term *academic dishonesty*). Introna and Hayes (2011) have done outstanding work to surface how this works against the interests of particular, often more vulnerable, groups such as international students. The surveillance practices instantiated in plagiarism detection and the language used may encourage the subversiveness and disobedience they seek to eradicate by fostering "attitudes of ill-will, skepticism, and distrust by signaling suspicion" (McEvily, Perrone, and Zaheer 2003, 99).

Zwagerman (2008) describes plagiarism detection as a "crusade against academic dishonesty" that is more damaging to the ideals of academia than cheating (677) and "diverts us from developing a pedagogy that encourages students' authentic engagement with words and ideas" (682). Indeed, at least one element of the design of good tasks—to encourage learning and enable assessment—is to design out plagiarism and other forms of academic practice that reduce the student's effort expended and challenge experienced by the student (Carroll 2002; Macdonald and Carroll 2006). Active thinking around the task is the foundation of good learning through assessment, and the direction of that processing will determine what is learned. If the nature of the task is such that subcontracting that task is possible, then the student has a choice: to accept the task as set and work hard to address it or to find a workaround to reduce the effort needed. The teacher can then deploy screening technology to ensure that should the latter route be chosen, the student will be caught. In the face of this algorithmic screening, the student still has a choice: to ignore the screening and work on the task or pay attention to the screening and work to circumvent it. What will be learned in the latter case will have little to do with the intended learning outcome of the original task.

Zwagerman goes further, arguing that a routine of plagiarism detection "reinforces rather than interrogates social roles and power differentials [and is] hostile toward critical thinking" (693). He argues persuasively that the use of plagiarism detection software sends entirely unhelpful messages about student work. Requiring students to submit their writing to a commercial service before a teacher even sees it "tells students that the first thing we look for in their work is evidence of cheating" (694). Introna (2016), in his work on algorithmic surveillance, judges this to be part of a commodification of academic writing:

> The academic essay (with its associated credits) is enacted as the site of economic exchange—academic writing for credit, credit for degree, degree for employment, and so forth. Within such a rationality, academic writing is an important commodity whose originality (or ownership) needs to be ensured—that is, against the unoriginal copy, presented fraudulently. (33)

As Gneezy and Rustichini (2000) found in their work on social and economic contracts, goodwill lost by making what was a relationship of trust into an economic contract cannot be regained. Institutions engaging in the commodification of student work through processes of plagiarism detection put teacher-student relationships of trust at great risk. Our own approach to this issue has been a clear and sustained refusal to use routine plagiarism detection systems in our own teaching, despite these being normalized within our institution.

Townley and Parsell (2004) critique the assumption that plagiarism is a problem of technology and therefore requires a technical solution. Instead, they argue that plagiarism arises because of a "failure of community," where academic values and attitudes are not being transferred from teachers to students (276). The reinvigoration of concepts of trust—and the importance of distinguishing them from untrusting practices of transparency and surveillance—will require action on the part of teachers to build and support academic communities in which trust is an underpinning.

Returning to Baier's definition of trust as necessary because "no one is able by herself to look after everything," we might reflect on the nature of the teaching assemblage created by the algorithm and the human together. Outsourcing some of our cognitive functions to a person or a technology requires some fundamental investment of trust in that person or technology. Should teachers trust plagiarism detection software to be a partner with them in shaping students' relationship to higher education—and to their own writing? Is the understanding of teaching that it manifests one that we support?

We would argue that it is not. We believe that plagiarism detection brings the algorithm and the human together in a teaching assemblage that is aligned with ethically unsound surveillance cultures in the university, and as teachers, we need to be much more attentive and critical about our own academic conduct in this regard. We suggest that teaching should not base itself in the foundations of distrust and commodification embodied by the plagiarism detection system, but should rather focus on building strong communities of trust and reciprocity within which students are motivated to learn. **A routine of plagiarism detection structures-in distrust.**

Snapshot

In 2016, the University of Melbourne in Australia announced the launch of a new pilot: the Cadmus system, developed by researchers based at the university. Cadmus offered something different from the postsubmission scanning of plagiarism detection software like Turnitin: it could monitor students' keystroke patterns, location, and other data while they wrote their assignments. Using a bespoke, authenticated environment, Cadmus could report on suspicious patterns of copying and pasting, for example, or writing being done from unusual locations or using keystroke patterns that suggested someone other than the appropriate person was writing, and therefore stamp out the possibility of students' subcontracting their assignment preparation. Students were quick to respond to this development, setting up the "Cadmus: not on my campus" petition and objecting to the intrusiveness of this monitoring and its undermining of academic freedom, alongside questions around data collection and possible issues with assistive and other devices that some students needed. As of the time of writing, trials of Cadmus continue.

CONCLUSION: STRATEGIES OF FUTURE MAKING

The chapters in this part of the book have made explicit connections between surveillance and trust, exploring the problems that come when, through surveillance and monitoring technologies, educational institutions fail to properly value the concept of trust as a mode of organization.

Online courses are prone to cultures of surveillance. Visibility is a pedagogical and ethical issue.

A routine of plagiarism detection structures-in distrust.

It is increasingly being argued—for example, in relation to the emergence of cryptocurrencies—that the direction of travel for a functioning society relies on trustless systems: those that are risk free because they do not require human judgment or negotiation, instead relying on unbreakable, perfect recording and visibility of financial or other transactions (Schaub et al. 2016). The desirability of this "trustlessness" is in sharp contrast with many decades of research into, for example, the place of collaboration, reciprocity, and sociality in human society (Wright 2001). As O'Neill (2002) has argued, it is ultimately not possible to eliminate the need for trust, only to move it further along some chain of accountability. These locations and processes of accountability are where we must turn our attention in order to understand the implications of technologies of visibility and monitoring for higher education.

Calls for more digital literacy, or better legal protection for personal data, do relatively little to address the ethics of trust that are so urgently in need of attention. The concept of a safe online space or a digital sanctuary is attracting increasing attention (Collier 2017), and our own recent research has emphasized the significant social value for students of surveillance-resistant anonymity in digital spaces (Bayne et al. 2019). However, what unmonitored spaces might exist in campus-based environments risk being eroded with the introduction of biometric monitoring and other facets of the data-intensive, "smart" campus (JISC 2017) that seek to make the concept of "off the record" defunct. At the same time, individual acts of subversion—attempts to limit visibility—become less possible within a surveillant campus culture built around monitoring, performance, and transparency. This is not just a problem for digital educators: the higher education community as a whole ignores it at our peril.

However, to address the issues raised in this part, we must be careful not to suggest that the answer lies in a return to an earlier time (before digital platforms, when class sizes were smaller and colleges served a more homogeneous population of students). Nostalgia will not help us to resist the dangers that would accompany a trustless higher education system. Instead, we must move toward digital futures for higher education that do not have surveillance at their heart. This is profoundly challenging work but ethically and pedagogically necessary.

At a macrolevel, the 2018 introduction in Europe of the General Data Protection Regulation (GDPR) is putting the onus on all data-gathering organizations, including colleges and universities, to reflect on, minimize, and deal ethically with the data they gather and hold about individuals. Such reimaginings of privacy, the right to be forgotten, the importance of context, and the limits citizens should be able to place on how visible they are offer real possibilities for higher education. At the microlevel, our work with master's students on our online distance program in digital education explores the potential impacts of learning analytics by making data visible to students in new ways that are rapidly easy to grasp (see Knox 2017b). When we make the extent of the data they generate clear to students, they express anxiety, fear of judgment, and resistance to what they see as inaccurate or unexpected reflections of their engagement.

Research into student responses to plagiarism detection software has shown that students understand its required use to be equivalent to an accusation of cheating or dishonesty (Penketh and Beaumont 2014, 100). When students comply with these practices or sign off on their use through accepting terms and conditions, that should not be taken as active, informed consent. As Lyon (2017) points out, normalization of surveillance and the erosion of expectations of privacy are central components of compliance with such practices. An effective strategy of resistance will include finding ways to resensitize ourselves and our students to the values we want to prioritize in our classrooms and offering means by which students can voice their responses to surveillance cultures in higher education.

A second important dimension of resistance is how we address these issues at strategic levels within our institutions and the sector more widely. There is a problem of leadership in digital education when significant decisions about technology practices are made on the basis that they are technical rather than pedagogical, cultural, or ethical. For this reason, important critical discussions may not take place before major initiatives are launched.

Ultimately, movement on these issues will require collective action to design and make real new possibilities for trust at scale, at a distance, and in the context of allowing students more freedom to be less visible. Along the way, we can correct some of the problematic assumptions that make surveillance practices seem so necessary: that face-to-face, small-scale classrooms are the only places where relationships of trust can flourish (see part IV); that making individuals' behavior, movement, and activity visible is a good substitute for those trusting relationships; and that desires to capture, record, and monitor can be deployed benevolently. We might, while we are at it, explore and challenge damaging assumptions that students are at college to game the system and seek more optimistic framings of students as willing partners within a community of education built around trust.

CONCLUSION

Figure 21.1

Our manifesto offers a challenge to what we see as some of the dominant and negative trajectories in digital education practices, politics, and technologies. Much of this book has been framed around the need to debunk, rethink, challenge, and stop "going further in the same way as before" (Latour 2010, 473). We have used the manifesto as a way of pushing against perspectives and assumptions that we see as undercritiqued, underpracticed, undertheorized, or underresearched. However, the manifesto is also intended to work positively as a statement of hope for a near future for education that is responsible, intellectually ambitious, critical, and creative. It is this spirit that drives the manifesto and that we have also tried to expand in this book.

The field is fast changing. When we reworked the 2011 manifesto in 2016, we kept several of the points and preoccupations presented in the earlier version—for example, around assessment, contact, multimodality, openness, and surveillance. But there were also many new points that aimed to address what we then saw as some of the key challenges and issues facing us as teachers: instrumentalist lockdown, neglect of materiality, at-scale teaching, algorithms, and automation. Looking ahead to the planned 2021 edition, we see the need to include much that is again new. We therefore use this conclusion to outline the trajectories that are likely to shape the next manifesto, looking ahead to advocate in new ways for how we, as teachers, we might work to shape a desirable near future for our teaching.

CLIMATE CRISIS

The next manifesto needs to address the implications for teaching about the climate crisis. What would our teaching, our colleges and universities, look like if we were to prioritize climate issues across all our work? One aspect of this relates to the greater focus on materiality we have argued for throughout this book: if we use digital technologies in our teaching, we need to pay attention not only to their social effects but to how they are made and the implications of their materiality. Vague statements around, for example, "clean tech" and "cloud-based" learning technologies will need to give way to important discussion about the massive ecological impact of the energy use, extraction, and waste disposal that underpin our everyday technology use.

In their assessment of future global emissions from the information and communication technologies (ICT) industry to 2040, Belkhir and Elmeligi (2018) found that the relative contribution of ICT to total global greenhouse emissions is expected to grow from about 1 percent in 2007 to 14 percent by 2040—more than half the contribution of the entire global transportation sector. Emissions from smartphone production are particularly concerning: the energy used for the manufacture and the gold and rare-earth elements needed to make them, the phone plans that encourage early replacement and obsolescence, the waste. But it is the server farms and data centers that power our devices and the software that drives them that make up the lion's share of ICT industry climate impact. According to Belkhir and Elmeligi, these infrastructural elements will contribute 45 percent of the overall ICT footprint by 2020 (459).

Beyond the infrastructural and industry aspects of the climate crisis, there is a need for a shared rethinking of education on the part of practitioners and leaders—a shift into a cultural mode focused on justice, planetary health, and sustainability. The ecoversities alliance, for example, is a translocal gathering of people from India, Mexico, Portugal, Canada, Zimbabwe, and elsewhere focused on asking, "What might the university look like if it were at the service of our diverse ecologies, cultures, economies, spiritualities and Life within our planetary home?" (ecoversities, n.d.)—a reimagining that takes account not only of climate issues but of social justice, radical pedagogy, cultural diversity, and decolonization. Similar ideas, differently framed but more specific to digital education, find their way into other gatherings, such as the Digital Pedagogy Lab with its focus on critical and liberatory pedagogies (Digital Pedagogy Lab, n.d.).

DATAFICATION

The datafication of society extends to all aspects of daily life and has implications for education across all sectors: the data trails we generate in our everyday lives; the surveillance and performance measurement regimes that feed on these; data-driven decision-making by institutions, governments, and corporations; and the concentration of influence in particular algorithms and platforms. We have included some discussion of these in this book, particularly in parts III and V, but we see this issue as having a much more central focus for a future manifesto.

Datafication in higher education converges with a range of social factors running in parallel with technological change— for example, unbundling and privatization (discussed below), changing patterns of engagement and recruitment at the global scale, the normalization of surveillance, the massification of higher education and its effects on staff workload and academic precarity, populism and the public perception of the value of universities. As Williamson (2019a) has argued, political imperatives to make universities instruments of social change, accompanied by the embedding of market values within higher education, mean that universities' data infrastructures are increasingly politicized, with practice becoming driven by performance metrics and strongly datafied evaluations of teaching and research quality.

In part V, we touched on the ethics and politics of the routine surveillance of students. With sensor- and device-based tracking of individuals technically possible and discussions around the "smart campus" becoming commonplace in universities, we teachers need to continue to develop ways of articulating a values-based position on student tracking, attendance, and engagement monitoring. This should be a position that recognizes where there are benefits as well as dangers. Predictive uses of data are already used in universities—for example, the combination of application and progression data sets to predict patterns of admission and withdrawal and analytics designed to identify students at risk of failure (see Dawson et al. 2017); however, the risks of predictive analytics and algorithmic discrimination are well documented, in education and elsewhere (O'Neil 2016). We need to keep a strong focus on the recoding of education discussed in part III, one that holds this intensification of data-driven planning and decision-making to account.

UNBUNDLING

"Unbundling" refers to the disaggregation of higher education into its component parts (for example, the separation of teaching from research; the outsourcing of student support and assessment; the breaking down of academic work into para-academic service roles). Fueled by the for-profit sector and happening as the expansion of higher education drives up the cost for governments and individuals, proponents of unbundling see in it a positive disruption that will make higher education more market driven and ultimately more affordable, with a greater focus on employability, flexibility, and personalization. MOOCs and the various new credit models emerging from these as they evolve are one example of unbundling, as are the promotion of fast-track degrees and more modular, flexible, professionally oriented provision (Wicklow 2017).

Criticism of unbundling focuses on its reduction of higher education to a service industry for employers, the undermining of the ideal of higher education for the public good, and its division of teaching from research. This division, it has been argued, pushes universities into impoverished, transmission-based teaching models isolated from the research leading edge (McCowan 2017). Important work from a project on the unbundled university in South Africa (Swinnerton et al. 2018) shows how unbundling works to reinforce existing power asymmetries, at the same time as it foregrounds fundamental discussions about the purpose and future of universities (Swartz et al. 2018).

Unbundling, taken to its logical end point, would indeed mean the end of universities as we know them: coherent, valued communities of scholarship in which research and teaching are supported in the interest of a social, inclusive vision that extends beyond the imperatives of the market. Unbundling very much needs its own call to attention.

ARTIFICIAL INTELLIGENCE

To a very large extent linked to datafication, advancements in artificial intelligence (AI) and automation have profound and growing implications for education. Our reference to robot colleagues in the 2016 manifesto (discussed in part III) was intended to be a playful way of indicating the need to remain open to the opportunities presented by AI in education while maintaining a critical perspective on it. However, as the AIEd industry grows—recent published reports describe an annual growth of 38 percent and a US$2 billion market by 2023 (Reuters 2019)—and the hype around personalized learning and AI tutors persists, we will need increasing nuance in the way we talk about the implications of this for teachers and teaching.

If AI has the potential to work well alongside human teachers (for example, by offering us new ways to analyze and direct student discussions in group forums or developing responsible new ways of building curriculum), it also eases us into an acceptance of automation highly problematic in a sector where precarious employment is rife. The path to automation is made easy where teacher professionalism is not valued and teaching itself has been reduced to low-grade, routinized work.

NEUROTECHNOLOGY

Neuroscience, and the insights it offers for the embodied and physiological dimensions of cognition, are likely to have a new impact on teaching and on the project of education itself in the coming years. Neurotechnology is another, and even more intimate, manifestation of the datafication discussed previously, defined by Williamson (2019b) as a broad field of brain-centred research and development dedicated to opening up the brain to computational analysis, modification, simulation and control. It includes advanced neural imaging systems for real-time brain monitoring; brain-inspired "neural networks" and bio-mimetic "cognitive computing"; synthetic neurobiology; brain-computer interfaces and wearable neuroheadsets; brain simulation platforms; neurostimulator systems; personal neuroinformatics; and other forms of brain-machine integration. (65)

This is another rapidly growing industry, with profound implications for teaching and learning, yet it remains under-discussed among teachers, often perceived as only marginally relevant. Of the many forms of neurotechnology that Williamson indicated, some are focused on enhancement. Transcranial direct current simulation, for example, is a cheap, low-tech procedure that involves sending a low electric current to the brain with apparently positive effects on memory and learning (Au et al. 2016). Others are more oriented to neurosensing and monitoring, such as the Harvard spin-out BrainCo, which has "developed a headband that reports real-time brainwave data to a teacher's dashboard to indicate levels of attention and engagement" (Williamson 2019b, 76). This kind of real-time monitoring opens up other possibilities for mining the mind, "not only to infer mental preferences, but also to prime, imprint or trigger those preferences" (Ienca and Adorno 2017, quoted in Williamson 2019b).

Educational neurotechnologies are surrounded by transhumanist "enhancement" imaginaries that are too easy to dismiss as sci-fi. They are real, promising to render individual, personal learning data more intrusive and potentially problematic than anything currently discussed in the mainstream literature on learning analytics and educational data. This is an issue for teaching practice that we need to surface and discuss.

FINALLY

The manifesto has always benefited from the insights, comments, and criticisms it has received from scholars all over the world on social media or in the many workshops, talks, and seminars we have given. We hope that this will continue and open up an invitation to everyone who has a stake in digital education—in whatever form—to engage with us as we shape the next version. We see this as collective work that extends well beyond the team in Edinburgh. We thank everyone who has contributed to its development so far and invite further comments, proposals, and provocations as we work on the next one. Digital education is, as John Urry has described futures research, "a murky world, but it is one that we have to enter, interrogate and hopefully re-shape" (Urry 2016, 192). Please join us as we continue to build The Manifesto for Teaching Online in this spirit.

REFERENCES

Adam, T. 2019. "Digital Neocolonialism and Massive Open Online Courses (MOOCs): Colonial Pasts and Neoliberal Futures." *Learning, Media and Technology* 44, no. 3: 365–380. https://doi.org/10.1080/17439884 .2019.1640740.

Adami, E. 2012. "The Rhetoric of the Implicit and the Politics of Representation in the Age of Copy-and-Paste." *Learning, Media and Technology* 37, no. 2: 131–144. https://doi.org/10.1080/17439884.2011.641567.

Archer, A. 2011. "Clip-Art or Design: Exploring the Challenges of Multimodal Texts for Writing Centres in Higher Education." *Southern African Linguistics and Applied Language Studies* 29, no. 4: 387–399. https://doi.org/ 10.2989/16073614.2011.651938.

Ashworth, J., and T. Ransom. 2019. "Has the College Wage Premium Continued to Rise? Evidence from Multiple U.S. Surveys." *Economics of Education Review* 69:149–154. https://doi.org/10.1016/j.econedurev .2019.02.003.

Atkins, D. E., J. Seely Brown, and A. L. Hammond. 2007. "A Review of the Open Educational Resources (OER) Movement: Achievements, Challenges, and New Opportunities." Report to the William and Flora Hewlett Foundation. http://www.hewlett.org/uploads/files/Hewlett _OER_report.pdf.

Au, J., B. Katz, M. Buschkuehl, K. Bunarjo, T. Senger, C. Zabel, S. M. Jaeggi, and J. Jonides. 2016. "Enhancing Working Memory Training with Transcranial Direct Current Stimulation." *Journal of Cognitive Neuroscience* 28, no. 9: 1419–1432. https://www.mitpressjournals.org/doi/10.1162/jocn_a_00979.

Baier, A. 1986. "Trust and Antitrust." *Ethics* 96, no. 2: 231–260. https://doi.org/10.1086/292745.

Bali, M., M. Crawford, R. Jessen, P. Signorelli, and M. Zamora. 2015. "What Makes a cMOOC Community Endure? Multiple Participant Perspectives from Diverse cMOOCs." *Educational Media International* 52, no. 2: 100–115. https://doi.org/10.1080/09523987.2015.1053290.

Bali, M., and S. Sharma. 2017. "Envisioning Postcolonial MOOCs: Critiques and Ways Forward." In *MOOCs and Higher Education: What Went Right, What Went Wrong and Where To Next?* edited by R. Bennet and M. Kent, 26–44. London: Routledge.

Barber, M., K. Donnelly, and S. Rizvi. 2013. *An Avalanche Is Coming: Higher Education and the Revolution Ahead.* Institute for Public Policy Research: Pearson.

Barlow, J. P. 1996. "A Declaration of the Independence of Cyberspace." Electronic Frontier Foundation. https://www.eff.org/cyberspace-independence.

Barneveld, A.v., K. E. Arnold, and J. P. Campbell. 2012. "Analytics in Higher Education." ELI Paper 1. Educause Learning Initiative,

Bateman, J. 2008. *Multimodality and Genre: A Foundation for the Systematic Analysis of Multimodal Documents.* Basingstoke: Palgrave Macmillan.

Bayne, S. 2006. "Temptation, Trash and Trust: The Authorship and Authority of Digital Texts." *E-Learning* 3, no. 1: 16–26. https://doi.org/10.2304/elea.2006.3.1.16.

Bayne, S. 2015a. "What's the Matter with 'Technology-Enhanced Learning'?" *Learning, Media and Technology* 40, no. 1: 5–20. https://doi.org/10.1080/17439884.2014.915851.

Bayne, S. 2015b. "Teacherbot: Interventions in Automated Teaching." *Teaching in Higher Education* 20, no. 4: 455–467. https://doi.org/10.1080/13562517.2015.1020783.

Bayne, S. 2016. "Posthumanism and Research in Digital Education." In *SAGE Handbook of E-Learning Research*, 2nd ed., edited by C. Haythornthwaite, J. Fransman, R. Andrews, and E. Meyers, 82–100. London: Sage.

Bayne, S. 2018. "Posthumanism: A Navigation Aid for Educators." *On Education: Journal for Research and Debate* 1, no. 2. https://www.oneducation.net/no-02-september-2018/posthumanism-a-navigation-aid-for-educators/.

Bayne, S., L. Connelly, C. Grover, N. Osborne, R. Tobin, E. Beswick, and L. Rouhani. 2019. "The Social Value of Anonymity on Campus: A Study of the Decline of Yik Yak." *Learning, Media and Technology* 44, no. 2: 92–107. https://doi.org/10.1080/17439884.2019.1583672.

Bayne, S., M. S. Gallagher, and J. Lamb. 2014. "Being 'at' University: The Social Topologies of Distance Students." *Higher Education* 67, no. 5: 569–583. https://doi.org/10.1007/s10734-013-9662-4.

Bayne, S., J. Knox, and J. Ross. 2015. "Open Education: The Need for a Critical Approach." *Learning, Media and Technology* 40, no. 3: 247–250. https://doi.org/10.1080/17439884.2015.1065272.

Bayne, S., and J. Ross. 2011. "'Digital Native' and 'Digital Immigrant' Discourses: A Critique." In *Digital Difference: Perspectives on Online Learning*, edited by R. Land and S. Bayne, 159–169. Rotterdam: Sense.

Bayne, S., and J. Ross. 2013. "Posthuman Literacy in Heterotopic Space: A Pedagogical Proposal." In *Literacy in the Digital University: Critical Perspectives on Learning, Scholarship, and Technology*, edited by R. Goodfellow and M. R. Lea, 95–110. London: Routledge.

Beer, D. 2017. "The Social Power of Algorithms." *Information, Communication, and Society* 20, no. 1: 1–13. https://doi.org/10.1080/1369118X.2016.1216147.

Bekele, T. A. 2010. "Motivation and Satisfaction in Internet-Supported Learning Environments: A Review." *Educational Technology and Society* 13, no. 2: 116–127.

Belkhir, L. and Elmeligi, A. 2018. "Assessing ICT Global Emissions Footprint: Trends to 2040 and Recommendations." *Journal of Cleaner Production* 177:448–463. https://doi.org/10.1016/j.jclepro.2017.12.239.

Bennett, S., K. Maton, and L. Kervin. 2008. "The 'Digital Natives' Debate: A Critical Review of the Evidence." *British Journal of Educational Technology* 39, no. 5: 321–331.

Berlin, I. 1969. *Four Essays on Liberty*. London: Oxford University Press.

Bezemer J. 2012. "What Is Multimodality?" University College London. https://mode.ioe.ac.uk/2012/02/16/what-is-multimodality/.

Bezemer, J., and G. Kress. 2008. "Writing in Multimodal Texts: A Social Semiotic Account of Designs for Learning." *Written Communication* 25, no. 2: 166–195. https://doi.org/10.1177/0741088307313177.

Bezemer, J., and G. Kress. 2016. *Multimodality, Learning and Communication: A Social Semiotic Frame*. Abingdon: Routledge.

Bickmore, L., and R. Christiansen. 2010. "Who Will Be the Inventors? Why Not Us?" Multimodal Compositions in the Two-Year College Classroom." *Teaching English in the Two-Year College* 37, no. 3: 230–242.

Biesta, G. 2005. "Against Learning: Reclaiming a Language for Education in an Age of Learning." *Nordisk Pedagogik* 24, no. 1: 54–66.

Biesta, G. 2012. "Giving Teaching Back to Education: Responding to the Disappearance of the Teacher." *Phenomenology and Practice* 6, no. 2: 35–49.

Biesta, G. 2017. *The Rediscovery of Teaching*. Abingdon: Routledge.

Birth, K. 2012. *Objects of Time: How Things Shape Temporality*. Basingstoke: Palgrave Macmillan.

BIS (Department for Business, Innovation and Skills). 2016. *Success as a Knowledge Economy: Teaching Excellence, Social Mobility and Student Choice*. London: Business, Innovation and Skills.

Blair, C. H. 2011. "Panic and Plagiarism: Authorship and Academic Dishonesty in a Remix Culture." *MediaTropes* 2, no. 1: 159–192.

Bolton, P., and S. Hubble. 2018. "Returns to a Degree." House of Commons Library briefing paper 8389, September 19.

Bourelle, A., T. Bourelle, and N. Jones. 2015. "Multimodality in the Technical Communication Classroom: Viewing Classical Rhetoric through a 21st Century Lens." *Technical Communication Quarterly* 24, no. 4: 306–327. https://doi.org/10.1080/10572252.2015.1078847.

boyd, d., and K. Crawford. 2012. "Critical Questions for Big Data: Provocations for a Cultural, Technological and Scholarly Phenomenon." *Information, Communication and Society* 15, no. 5: 662–679. https://doi.org/10.1080/1369118X.2012.678878.

Boys, J. 2016. "Finding the Spaces In-Between: Learning as a Social Material Practice." In *Place-Based Spaces for Networked Learning*, edited by L. Carvalho, P. Goodyear, and M. de Laat, 59–72. London: Routledge.

Breslow, L., D. E. Pritchard, J. DeBoer, G. S. Stump, A. D. Ho, and D. T. Seaton. 2013. "Studying Learning in the Worldwide Classroom: Research into edX's First MOOC." *Research and Practice in Assessment* 8, no. 2: 13–25.

Brown, C., and L. Czerniewicz. 2010. "Debunking the 'Digital Native': Beyond Digital Apartheid, towards Digital Democracy." *Journal of Computer Assisted Learning* 26:357–369. https://doi.org/10.1111/j.1365-2729.2010.00369.x.

Brown, J. S., and R. P. Adler. 2008. "Minds on Fire: Open Education, the Long Tail, and Learning 2.0." *Educause Review* 43:16–32.

Browne, J. 2010. "Securing a Sustainable Future for Higher Education: An Independent Review of Higher Education Funding and Student Finance." https://www.gov.uk/government/publications/the-browne-report-higher-education-funding-and-student-finance.

Buchanan, R. 2011. "Paradox, Promise and Public Pedagogy: Implications of the Federal Government's Digital Education Revolution." *Australian Journal of Teacher Education* 36, no. 2: 67–78. https://doi.org/10.14221/ajte.2011v36n2.6.

Camilleri, A., U. Ehlers, and J. Pawlowski. 2014. *State of the Art Review of Quality Issues Related to Open Educational Resources (OER)*. Luxembourg: Office of the European Union.

Campbell, J. P., P. B. De Blois, and D. G. Oblinger. 2007. "Academic Analytics: A New Tool for a New Era." *Educause Review* 42, no. 4: 40–57.

"Cape Town Open Education Declaration." 2007. http://www.capetowndeclaration.org/read-the-declaration.

Carpenter, R. 2014. "Negotiating the Spaces of Design in Multimodal Composition." *Computers and Composition* 33:68–78. https://doi.org/10.1016/j.compcom.2014.07.006.

Carroll, J. 2002. *A Handbook for Deterring Plagiarism in Higher Education.* Oxford: Oxford Centre for Staff and Learning Development.

Caswell, T., S. Henson, M. Jensen, and D. Wiley. 2008. "Open Educational Resources: Enabling Universal Education." *International Review of Research in Open and Distance Learning* 9, no. 1. http://www.irrodl.org/index.php/irrodl/article/view/469/1001.

Caudle, J. D. 2016. "Spatial Context: How Can Digital Tools and Media Be Used to Spatio-Temporally Contextualize Learning in Online Learning Environments?" http://digital.education.ed.ac.uk/showcases/spatial_context/.

Clow, D. 2013. "An Overview of Learning Analytics." *Teaching in Higher Education* 18, no. 6: 683–695. https://doi.org/10.1080/13562517.2013.827653.

Colby, R. 2014. "Writing and Assessing Procedural Rhetoric in Student-Produced Video Games." *Computers and Composition* 31:43–52. https://doi.org/10.1016/j.compcom.2013.12.003.

Coldewey, D. 2017. "MOOC Enrollment Drops at HarvardX and MITx after Free Certifications Disappear." TechCrunch. https://techcrunch.com/2017/01/13/mooc-enrollment-drops-at-harvardx-and-mitx-after-free-certifications-disappear/.

Coleman, L. 2012. "Incorporating the Notion of Recontextualisation in Academic Literacies Research: The Case of a South African Vocational Web Design and Development Course." *Higher Education Research and Development* 31, no. 3: 325–338. https://doi.org/10.1080/07294360.2011.631519.

Collier, A. 2017. "Digital Sanctuary: Protection and Refuge on the Web?" *Educause Review* 52, no. 5: 56–57.

Conrads, J., M. Rasmussen, N. Winters, A. Geniet, L. Langer, C. Redecker, P. Kampylis, M. Bacigalupo, and Y. Punie. 2017. *Digital Education Policies in Europe and Beyond: Key Design Principles for More Effective Policies.* Brussels: European Commission.

Creative Commons. n.d. Accessed August 16, 2019, at https://creativecommons.org/.

Cronin, C., and I. MacLaren. 2018. "Conceptualising OEP: A Review of Theoretical and Empirical Literature in Open Educational Practices." *Open Praxis* 10, no. 2. https://doi.org/10.5944/openpraxis.10.2.825.

Daniel, J., and D. Killion. 2012. "Are Open Educational Resources the Key to Global Economic Growth?" *Guardian Online*, July 4. http://www.guardian.co.uk/higher-education-network/blog/2012/jul/04/open-educational-resources-and-economic-growth.

Davis, G. 2017. "Will Universities Become a Redundant Archipelago?" *Times Higher Education.* October 26. https://www.timeshighereducation.com/opinion/will-universities-become-redundant-archipelago.

Dawson, S., J. Jovanovic, D. Gašević, and A. Pardo. 2017. "From Prediction to Impact: Evaluation of a Learning Analytics Retention Program." In *Proceedings of the Seventh International Learning Analytics and Knowledge Conference*, 474–478. New York: ACM.

Deimann, M., and Farrow, R. 2013. "Rethinking OER and Their Use: Open Education as Bildung." *International Review of Research in Open and Distributed Learning* 14, no. 3.

Department for Education. 2019. "Post-18 Review of Education and Funding: Independent Panel Report." UK Department for Education. https://www.gov.uk/government/publications/post-18-review-of-education-and-funding-independent-panel-report.

Digital Pedagogy Lab. n.d. Accessed August 16, 2019, at http://www.digitalpedagogylab.com/about/.

Dillenbourg, P. 2016. "The Evolution of Research on Digital Education." *International Journal of Artificial Intelligence in Education* 26, no. 2: 544–560. https://doi.org/10.1007/s40593-016-0106-z.

Dima, A. M., L. Beug, M. D. Vasilescu, and M. A. Maanen. 2018. "The Relationship between the Knowledge Economy and Global Competitiveness in the European Union." *Sustainability* 10, no. 6: 1–15.

Dreyfus, H. L. 2001. *On the Internet.* London: Routledge.

Dumford, A. D., and A. L. Miller. 2018. "Online Learning in Higher Education: Exploring Advantages and Disadvantages for Engagement." *Journal of Computing in Higher Education* 30, no. 3: 452–465.

Eagleman, D. 2011. *Incognito: The Secret Lives of the Brain.* New York: Pantheon.

ecoversities. n.d. Accessed August 16, 2019, at http://ecoversities.org/.

Edwards, R. 2015. "Knowledge Infrastructures and the Inscrutability of Openness in Education." *Learning, Media and Technology* 40, no. 3: 251–264.

Edwards, R., and P. Carmichael. 2012. "Secret Codes: The Hidden Curriculum of Semantic Web Technologies." *Discourse: Studies in the Cultural Politics of Education* 33, no. 4: 575–590. https://doi.org/10.1080/01596306.2012.692963.

Edwards, R., and T. Fenwick. 2015. "Critique and Politics: A Sociomaterialist Intervention." *Educational Philosophy and Theory* 47, no. 13–14: 1385–1404.

Edwards, R., F. Tracy, and K. Jordan. 2011. "Mobilities, Moorings and Boundary Marking in Developing Semantic Technologies in Educational Practices." *Research in Learning Technology* 19, no. 3: 219–232.

edX. n.d.a. "MicroMasters." Accessed August 16, 2019, at https://www.edx.org/micromasters.

edX. n.d.b. "u.lab: Leading from the Emerging Future." Accessed August 16, 2019, at https://www.edx.org/course/u-lab-leading-emerging-future-mitx-15-671-1x-0.

edX. 2014. U.Lab: Transforming Business, Society, and Self. MITx on edX. About Video. (Video.) https://www.youtube.com/watch?v=gF8wV9OlUHc.

Ellaway, R. H., J. Coral, D. Topps, and M. Topps. 2015. "Exploring Digital Professionalism." *Medical Teacher* 37, no. 9: 844–849. https://doi.org/10.3109/0142159X.2015.1044956.

Enbar, A. 2016. "Higher Education Is Broken, But There's Still Hope for the Future." *Forbes,* August 26. https://www.forbes.com/sites/quora/2016/08/26/higher-education-is-broken-but-theres-still-hope-for-the-future/#1d29362c209d.

Engel, L. C., and M. M. Siczek. 2018. "A Cross-National Comparison of International Strategies: Global Citizenship and the Advancement of National Competitiveness." *Compare: A Journal of Comparative and International Education* 48, no. 5: 749–767. https://doi.org/10.1080/03057925.2017.1353408.

Eubanks, V. 2018. *Automating Inequality: How High-Tech Tools Profile, Police, and Punish the Poor.* New York: St. Martin's Press.

European Commission. 2018. "Speech by Commissioner Gabriel on Building the European Digital Economy and Society at the DLD Conference." January 22. http://europa.eu/rapid/press-release_SPEECH-18-390_en.htm.

Feenberg, A., and C. Xin. 2010. "What Is Facilitation?" DPH (February). http://base.d-p-h.info/en/fiches/dph/fiche-dph-8213.html.

Fenwick, T. 2010. "Re-Thinking the "Thing": Sociomaterial Approaches to Understanding and Researching Learning in Work." *Journal of Workplace Learning* 22, no. 1: 104–116.

Fenwick, T., and R. Edwards. 2010. *Actor-Network Theory in Education.* London: Routledge.

Fenwick, T., R. Edwards, and P. Sawchuk. 2011. *Emerging Approaches to Educational Research: Tracing the Sociomaterial.* London: Routledge.

Fenwick, T., and P. Landri. 2012. "Materialities, Textures and Pedagogies: Socio-Material Assemblages in Education." *Pedagogy, Culture and Society* 20, no. 1: 1–7.

Ferguson, R. 2012. "Learning Analytics: Drivers, Developments and Challenges." *International Journal of Technology Enhanced Learning* 4, no. 5/6: 304–317.

Fischer, G. 2014. "Beyond Hype and Underestimation: Identifying Research Challenges for the Future of MOOCs." *Distance Education* 35, no. 2: 149–158.

Fitzpatrick, K. 2011a. "Kathleen Fitzpatrick: 'The Future of Authorship: Writing in the Digital Age.'" YouTube. (Video.) https://www.youtube.com/watch?v=v4qq01Qskv0.

Fitzpatrick, K. 2011b. "The Digital Future of Authorship: Rethinking Originality." *Culture Machine* 12:1–26. https://culturemachine.net/wp-content/uploads/2019/01/6-The-Digital-433-889-1-PB.pdf.

Foucault, M. 1977. "What Is an Author?" In *Language, Counter-Memory, Practice: Selected Essays and Interviews*, edited by D. F. Bouchard and translated by D. F. Bouchard and S. Simon, 113–138. Ithaca, NY: Cornell University Press.

Friesen, N. 2019. "The Technological Imaginary in Education, or: Myth and Enlightenment in 'Personalised Learning.'" In *The Digital Age and Its Discontents*, edited by M. Stocchetti. Helsinki: University of Helsinki Press.

FUN-MOOC. n.d.a. "About FUN." Accessed August 16, 2019, at https://www.fun-mooc.fr/about.

FUN-MOOC n.d.b. "Scientific Humanities—Session 1." Accessed August 2019, at https://www.fun-mooc.fr/courses/SciencesPo/05004/Trimestre_1_2014/about.

Gašević, D., S. Dawson, and G. Siemens. 2015. "Let's Not Forget: Learning Analytics Are about Learning." *TechTrends* 59, no. 1: 54–71.

Gewirtz, S., and A. Cribb. 2013. "Representing 30 Years of Higher Education Change: UK Universities and the Times Higher." *Journal of Educational Administration and History* 45, no. 1: 58–83.

Gillespie, T. 2014. "The Relevance of Algorithms." In *Media Technologies*, edited by T. Gillespie, P. Boczkowski, and K. Foot, 167–194. Cambridge, MA: MIT Press.

Giroux, H. 2017. "Pedagogy of the Precariat: Conversation with Petar Jandrić." In *Learning in the Age of Digital Reason*, edited by P. Jandrić, 139–157. Rotterdam: Sense.

Gneezy, U., and A. Rustichini. 2000. "A Fine Is a Price." *Journal of Legal Studies* 29, no. 1: 1–17. https://doi.org/10.1086/468061.

Goel, A., and L. Polepeddi. 2016. "Jill Watson: A Virtual Teaching Assistant for Online Education." Technical report, Georgia Institute of Technology. http://hdl.handle.net/1853/59104.

Gordon, N. 2014. *Flexible Pedagogies: Technology-Enhanced Learning*. York: Higher Education Academy.

Gourlay, L., and M. Oliver. 2013. "Beyond 'the Social': Digital Literacies as Sociomaterial Practice." In *Literacy in the Digital University: Critical Perspectives on Learning, Scholarship, and Technology*, edited by R. Goodfellow and M. R. Lea, 79–94. London: Routledge.

Groom, J. 2016. "Can We Imagine Tech Infrastructure as an OER? Or, Clouds, Containers, and APIs, Oh My!" Keynote address at the seventh Open Educational Resources Conference, University of Edinburgh. https://youtu.be/IFzZMOhkBNw.

Gunsberg, B. 2015. "The Evaluative Dynamics of Multimodal Composing." *Computers and Composition* 38:1–15. https://doi.org/10.1016/j.compcom.2015.09.002.

Hall, R. 2015. "For a Political Economy of Massive Open Online Courses." *Learning, Media and Technology* 40, no. 3: 265–286. https://doi.org/10.1080/17439884.2015.1015545.

Hall, R. 2016. "Technology-Enhanced Learning and Co-Operative Practice against the Neoliberal University." *Interactive Learning Environments* 24, no. 5: 1004–1015. https://doi.org/10.1080/10494820.2015.1128214.

Hamilton, E. C., and N. Friesen. 2013. "Online Education: A Science and Technology Studies Perspective." *Canadian Journal of Learning and Technology* 39, no. 2. http://cjlt.csj.ualberta.ca/index.php/cjlt/article/view/689.

Hammick, J. K., and M. J. Lee. 2014. "Do Shy People Feel Less Communication Apprehension Online? The Effects of Virtual Reality on the Relationship between Personality Characteristics and Communication Outcomes." *Computers in Human Behavior* 33, no. C: 302–310. https://doi.org/10.1016/j.chb.2013.01.046.

Hannam, K., M. Sheller, and J. Urry. 2006. "Editorial: Mobilities, Immobilities and Moorings." *Mobilities* 1, no. 1: 1–22.

Haraway, D. 1991. *Simians, Cyborgs and Women: The Reinvention of Nature*. New York: Routledge.

Hargittai, E. 2010. "Digital Na(t)ives? Variation in Internet Skills and Uses among Members of the 'Net Generation.'" *Sociological Inquiry* 80, no. 1: 92–113.

Harloe, M., and B. Perry. 2004. "Universities, Localities and Regional Development: The Emergence of the 'Mode 2' University?" *International Journal of Urban and Regional Research* 28, no. 1: 212–232.

Helsper, E. J., and R. Eynon. 2010. "Digital Natives: Where Is the Evidence?" *British Educational Research Journal* 36, no. 3: 503–520.

Henderikx, M. A., K. Kreijns, and M. Kalz. 2017. "Refining Success and Dropout in Massive Open Online Courses Based on the Intention–Behavior Gap." *Distance Education* 38, no. 3: 353–368. https://doi.org/10.1080/01587919.2017.1369006.

Herold, B. 2016. "Facebook's Zuckerberg to Bet Big on Personalized Learning." *Education Week*, March 7. https://www.edweek.org/ew/articles/2016/03/07/facebooks-zuckerberg-to-bet-big-on-personalized.html.

Hindman, M. 2018. *The Internet Trap: How the Digital Economy Builds Monopolies and Undermines Democracy*. Princeton, NJ: Princeton University Press. https://doi.org/10.1080/00131857.2014.930681.

Hodgkinson-Williams, C. A., and H. Trotter. 2018. "A Social Justice Framework for Understanding Open Educational Resources and Practices in the Global South." *Journal of Learning for Development* 5, no. 3. https://jl4d.org/index.php/ejl4d/article/view/312.

Hood, B. 2012. "Choreographing the Glitch." https://www.research.ed.ac.uk/portal/files/16205053/bhood_choreotheglitch_birm11_09_eWiC.pdf.

Huggins, S. 2017. "OEC Announces the Year of Open." Open Education Consortium. http://www.oeconsortium.org/2017/01/oec-announces-the-year-of-open/.

Ienca, M., and R. Andorno. 2017. "Towards New Human Rights in the Age of Neuroscience and Neurotechnology." *Life Sciences, Society and Policy* 13, no. 5: 1–27. https://doi.org/10.1186/s40504-017-0050-1.

Introna, L. D. 2016. "Algorithms, Governance, and Governmentality: On Governing Academic Writing." *Science, Technology, and Human Values* 41, no. 1: 17–49. https://doi.org/10.1177/0162243915587360.

Introna, L. D., and N. Hayes. 2011. "On Sociomaterial Imbrications: What Plagiarism Detection Systems Reveal and Why It Matters." *Information and Organization* 21, no. 2: 107–122. https://doi.org/10.1016/j.infoandorg.2011.03.001.

Jewitt, C. 2009. "An Introduction to Multimodality." In *The Routledge Handbook of Multimodal Analysis*, edited by C. Jewit, 14–27. London: Routledge.

JISC. 2017. *Intelligent Campus Guide*. Accessed November 17, 2019, at https://intelligentcampus.jiscinvolve.org/wp/intelligent-campus-guide/.

Johnson, D., and G. Kress. 2003. "Globalisation, Literacy and Society: Redesigning Pedagogy and Assessment." *Assessment in Education: Principles, Policy and Practice* 10, no. 1: 5–14. https://doi.org/10.1080/09695940301697.

Johnson, L., S. Adams Becker, M. Cummins, V. Estrada, A. Freeman, A., and C. Hall. 2016. *NMC Horizon Report: 2016 Higher Education Edition*. Austin, TX: New Media Consortium. https://www.learntechlib.org/p/171478/.

Johnson, L., S. Becker, V. Estrada, and A. Freeman. 2014. "NMC Horizon Report: 2014 Higher Education Edition." Austin, TX: New Media Consortium. https://www.learntechlib.org/p/130341/.

Johnson, L., S. Adams Becker, V. Estrada, and A. Freeman. 2015. "NMC Horizon Report: 2015 Higher Education Edition." Austin, TX: New Media Consortium. https://www.learntechlib.org/p/182010/.

Jones, C., R. Ramanau, S. Cross, and G. Healing. 2010. "Net Generation or Digital Natives: Is There a Distinct New Generation Entering University?" *Computers and Education* 54:722–732.

Jordan, K. 2014. "Initial Trends in Enrolment and Completion of Massive Open Online Courses." *International Review of Research in Open and Distributed Learning* 15:133–160. https://doi.org/10.19173/irrodl.v15i1.1651.

Kadianaki, I., and E. Andreouli. 2017. "Essentialism in Social Representations of Citizenship: An Analysis of Greeks' and Migrants' Discourse." *Political Psychology* 38, no. 5: 833–848. https://doi.org/10.1111/pops.12271.

Kalir, J. 2018. "Equity-Oriented Design in Open Education." *International Journal of Information and Learning Technology* 35, no. 5: 357–367. https://doi.org/10.1108/IJILT-06-2018-0070.

Kimber, K., and C. Wyatt-Smith. 2010. "Secondary Students' Online Use and Creation of Knowledge: Refocusing Priorities for Quality Assessment and Learning." *Australasian Journal of Education Technology* 26, no. 5: 607–625.

King, E., and R. Boyatt. 2015. "Exploring Factors That Influence Adoption of e-Learning within Higher Education." *British Journal of Educational Technology* 46, no. 6: 1272–1280. https://doi.org/10.1111/bjet.12195.

Knox, J. 2013a. "Five Critiques of the Open Educational Resources Movement." *Teaching in Higher Education* 18, no. 8: 821–832. https://doi.org/10.1080/13562517.2013.774354.

Knox, J. 2013b. "The Limitations of Access Alone: Moving towards Open Processes in Education." *Open Praxis* 5, no. 1:21–29.

Knox, J. 2016a. *Posthumanism and the MOOC: Contaminating the Subject of Global Education.* Abingdon: Routledge.

Knox, J. 2016b. "Posthumanism and the MOOC: Opening the Subject of Digital Education." *Studies in Philosophy and Education* 35, no. 3: 305–320. https://doi.org/10.1007/s11217-016-9516-5.

Knox, J. 2017a. "De-colonising the MOOC: A Critical View of the Platform Model for Global Education." Translated by Junhong Xiao. *Distance Education in China* 5. https://doi.org/10.13541/j.cnki.chinade.20170420.001.

Knox, J. 2017b. "Data Power in Education: Exploring Critical Awareness with the 'Learning Analytics Report Card' (LARC)." *Television and New Media* 18, no. 8: 734–752. https://doi.org/10.1177/1527476417690029.

Knox, J. 2018. "Beyond the 'c' and the 'x': Learning with Algorithms in Massive Open Online Courses (MOOCs)." *International Review of Education* 64, no. 2: 161–178. https://doi.org/10.1007/s11159-018-9707-0.

Knox, J., B. Williamson, and S. Bayne. 2019. "Machine Behaviourism: Future Visions of 'Learnification' and 'Datafication' across Humans and Digital Technologies." *Learning, Media and Technology* 45, no. 1: 31–45. https://doi.org/10.1080/17439884.2019.1623251.

Koller, D. 2012. "What We're Learning from Online Education." TED Talk. August 1. https://www.ted.com/talks/daphne_koller_what_we_re_learning_from_online_education.

Kramer, A. D. I., J. E. Guillory, and J. T. Hancock. 2014. "Experimental Evidence of Massive-Scale Emotional Contagion through Social Networks." *Proceedings of the National Academy of Sciences of the United States of America* 111, no. 24: 8788–8790.

Krause, M. B. 2013. "'A Series of Unfortunate Events': The Repercussions of Print-Literacy as the Only Literacy for Talented Boys." *Gifted Child Today* 36, no. 4: 236–245. https://doi.org/10.1177/1076217513501805.

Kress, G. 2005. "Gains and Losses: New Forms of Texts, Knowledge and Learning." *Computers and Composition* 22, no. 1: 5–22. https://doi.org/10.1016/j.compcom.2004.12.004.

Kress, G., and S. Selander. 2012. "Multimodal Design, Learning and Cultures of Recognition." *Internet and Higher Education* 15:265–268. https://doi.org/10.1016/j.iheduc.2011.12.003.

Kress, G., and T. van Leeuwen. 2001. *Multimodal Discourse: The Modes and Media of Contemporary Communication.* London: Hodder Arnold.

Kretsos, L., and I. Livanos. 2016. "The Extent and Determinants of Precarious Employment in Europe." *International Journal of Manpower* 37, no. 1: 25–43. https://doi/.org/10.1108/IJM-12-2014-0243.

Lamb, J. 2013. A Manifesto for Teaching Online, 2013 remix. (Video.) https://vimeo.com/77766791.

Lamb, J. 2017. Manifesto for Teaching Online, June 2017. (Video.) https://vimeo.com/222406740.

Lamb, J. 2018. "To Boldly Go: Feedback as Digital, Multimodal Dialogue." *Multimodal Technologies and Interaction* 2, no. 3: 49. https://doi.org/10.3390/mti2030049.

Lamb, J. n.d. "The Elektronisches Lernen Muzik Project." Accessed March 5, 2020, at https://www.elernenmuzik.net.

Lang, C., G. Siemens, A. Wise, and D. Gašević. 2017. *Handbook of Learning Analytics.* SoLAR. https://doi.org/10.18608/hla17.

Latour, B. 1999. *Pandora's Hope: Essays on the Reality of Science Studies.* Cambridge, MA: Harvard University Press.

Latour, B. 2010. "An Attempt at a 'Compositionist Manifesto.'" *New Literary History* 41, no. 3: 471–490.

Laurillard, D. 2008. "Open Teaching: The Key to Sustainable and Effective Open Education." In *Opening Up Education: The Collective Advancement of Education through Open Technology, Open Content, and Open Knowledge*, edited by T. Iiyoshi, and M. S. Vijay Kumar, 319–335. Cambridge, MA: MIT Press.

Law, J. 2004. *After Method: Mess in Social Science Research*. Abingdon: Routledge.

Lea, M. R., and S. Jones. 2011. "Digital Literacies in Higher Education: Exploring Textual and Technological Practice." *Studies in Higher Education* 36, no. 4: 377–393. https://doi.org/10.1080/03075071003664021.

Leckart, S. 2012. "The Stanford Education Experiment Could Change Higher Learning Forever." *Wired* (March). https://www.wired.com/2012/03/ff_aiclass/.

Levin, R. 2017. "Five Years after the Year of the MOOC: Where Are We Now?" Presented at the Plenary Keynote Session, EMOOCS 2017 Conference. (Video.) https://www.youtube.com/watch?v=0VoxL6lIX6g.

Littlejohn, A., and N. Hood. 2017. "How Educators Build Knowledge and Expand Their Practice: The Case of Open Education Resources." *British Journal of Educational Technology* 48:499–510. https://doi.org/10.1111/bjet.12438.

Lombard, M., and T. Ditton. 1997. "At the Heart of It All: The Concept of Presence." *Journal of Computer Mediated Communication* 3, no. 2. https://doi.org/10.1111/j.1083-6101.1997.tb00072.x.

Long, P., and G. Siemens. 2011. "Penetrating the Fog: Analytics in Learning and Education." *Educause Review* 46, no. 5: 31–40.

Lorenz, C. 2012. "If You're So Smart, Why Are You under Surveillance? Universities, Neoliberalism, and New Public Management." *Critical Inquiry* 38, no. 3: 599–629. https://doi.org/10.1086/664553.

Luckin, R., W. Holmes, M. Griffiths, L. B. Forcier. 2016. *Intelligence Unleashed: An Argument for AI in Education*. London: Pearson. https://static.googleusercontent.com/media/edu.google.com/en//pdfs/Intelligence-Unleashed-Publication.pdf.

Lukkarinen, A., P. Koivukangas, and T. Seppälä. 2016. "Relationship between Class Attendance and Student Performance." *Procedia—Social and Behavioral Sciences* 228:341–347. https://doi.org/10.1016/j.sbspro .2016.07.051.

Lynch, K. 2006. "Neo-Liberalism and Marketisation: The Implications for Higher Education." *European Educational Research Journal* 5, no. 1: 1–17. https://doi.org/10.2304/eerj.2006.5.1.1.

Lyon, D. 2017. "Surveillance Culture: Engagement, Exposure, and Ethics in Digital Modernity." *International Journal of Communication* 11: 824–842.

MacAllister, J. 2016. "What Should Educational Institutions Be For?" *British Journal of Educational Studies* 64, no. 3: 375–391. https://doi.org/ 10.1080/00071005.2015.1131811.

Macdonald, R., and J. Carroll. 2006. "Plagiarism—a Complex Issue Requiring a Holistic Institutional Approach." *Assessment and Evaluation in Higher Education* 31, no. 2: 233–245. https://doi.org/10.1080/ 02602930500262536.

Macfarlane, B. 2013. "The Surveillance of Learning: A Critical Analysis of University Attendance Policies." *Higher Education Quarterly* 67, no. 4: 358–373. https://doi.org/10.1111/hequ.12016.

Macfarlane, B. 2016. *Freedom to Learn*. Abingdon: Routledge.

Macintosh, W., R. McGreal, and J. Taylor. 2011. "Open Education Resources (OER) for Assessment and Credit for Students Project: Towards a Logic Model and Plan for Action." UNESCO Chair in Open Educational Resources. http://auspace.athabascau.ca:8080/dspace/handle/2149/3039.

Mackness, J. 2015. "Edinburgh University's Updated Manifesto for Teaching Online—2015." *Jenny Connected* (blog). https://jennymackness .wordpress.com/2015/10/21/edinburgh-universitys-updated-manifesto -for-teaching-online-2015/.

Mamdani, M. 2001. "Beyond Settler and Native as Political Identities: Overcoming the Political Legacy of Colonialism." *Comparative Studies in Society and History* 43, no. 4: 651–664.

Mander, J. 1978. *Four Arguments for the Elimination of Television*. New York: Morrow Quill.

"Manifesto for Teaching Online." 2011, 2016. https://blogs.ed.ac.uk/manifestoteachingonline/.

Markoff, J. 2011. "Virtual and Artificial, But 58,000 Want Course." *New York Times*, August 16. https://www.nytimes.com/2011/08/16/science/16stanford.html.

Marsh, B. 2004. "Turnitin.com and the Scriptural Enterprise of Plagiarism Detection." *Computers and Composition* 21, no. 4: 427–438. https://doi.org/10.1016/j.compcom.2004.08.

Massey, D. 2005. *Space, Place and Gender*. Minneapolis: University of Minnesota Press.

Massumi, B. 2015. *Politics of Affect*. Cambridge, UK: Polity Press.

Matson, J. 2011. "70,000 Students Flock to Free Online Course in Artificial Intelligence." *Scientific American* (blog). https://blogs.scientificamerican.com/observations/stanford-artificial-intelligence/.

Matthewman, S., and P. Triggs. 2004. "'Obsessive Compulsive Font Disorder': The Challenge of Supporting Pupils Writing with the Computer." *Computers and Education* 43, no. 1–2: 125–135. https://doi.org/10.1016/j.compedu.2003.12.015.

McAuley, A., B. Stewart, G. Siemens, and D. Cormier. 2010. *The MOOC Model for Digital Practice*. https://www.oerknowledgecloud.org/archive/MOOC_Final.pdf.

McCowan, T. 2017. "Higher Education, Unbundling, and the End of the University as We Know It." *Oxford Review of Education*, 43, no. 6: 733–748. https://doi.org/10.1080/03054985.2017.1343712.

McEvily, B., V. Perrone, and A. Zaheer. 2003. "Trust as an Organizing Principle." *Organization Science* 14, no. 1: 91–103. https://doi.org/10.1287/orsc.14.1.91.12814.

McKenna, C., and J. Hughes, J. 2013. "Values, Digital Texts, and Open Practices—a Changing Scholarly Landscape in Higher Education." In *Literacy in the Digital University: Critical Perspectives on Learning, Scholarship, and Technology*, edited by R. Goodfellow and M. R. Lea, 15–16. London: Routledge.

McKenna, C., and C. McAvinia. 2011. "Difference and Discontinuity—Making Meaning through Hypertexts." In *Digital Difference: Perspectives on Online Learning*, edited by R. Land and S. Bayne, 45–60. Rotterdam: Sense Publishers.

McKie, A. 2019. "1.3 Billion Turnitin Sale Spotlights Intellectual Property Fears." *Times Higher Education*, March 11.

McMillan Cottom, C. 2017. *Lower Ed: The Troubling Rise of For-Profit Colleges in the New Economy*. New York: New Press.

Miller, V. 2011. *Understanding Digital Culture*. London: Sage.

Milligan, C., and A. Littlejohn. 2014. "Supporting Professional Learning in a Massive Open Online Course." *International Review of Research in Open and Distance Learning* 15, no. 5: 197–213. https://doi.org/10.19173/irrodl.v15i5.1855.

Moffatt, M. P., and S. G. Rich. 1957. "Implications of Automation for Education." *Journal of Educational Sociology* 30, no. 6: 268–274. https://doi.org/10.2307/2264278.

Moisio, S., and A. Kangas. 2016. "Reterritorializing the Global Knowledge Economy: An Analysis of Geopolitical Assemblages of Higher Education." *Global Networks* 16, no. 3: 268–287.

Mol, A., and J. Law. 1994. "Regions, Networks and Fluids: Anaemia and Social Topology." *Social Studies of Science* 24, no. 4: 641–671. https://doi.org/10.1177/030631279402400402.

Moore, M. G. 2013. *Handbook of Distance Education*, 3rd ed. New York: Routledge.

Morris, S. M., and J. Stommel. 2017. "A Guide for Resisting EdTech: The Case against Turnitin." *Hybrid Pedagogy* 15. http://hybridpedagogy.org/resisting-edtech/.

Mphahlele, A., and S. McKenna. 2019. "The Use of Turnitin in the Higher Education Sector: Decoding the Myth." *Assessment and Evaluation in Higher Education* 44, no. 7: 1079–1089.

Munford, M. 2018. "Cryptocurrencies and the Blockchain: Q&A with Erik Finman, Teenage Whiz Kid." *Forbes*, January 22. https://www

.forbes.com/sites/montymunford/2018/01/22/cryptocurrencies-and-the
-blockchain-qa-with-erik-firman-teenage-whizz-kid/.

Munro, M. 2018. "The Complicity of Digital Technologies in the Marketisation of UK Higher Education: Exploring the Implications of a Critical
Discourse Analysis of Thirteen National Digital Teaching and Learning
Strategies." *International Journal of Educational Technology in Higher Education* 15, no. 11. https://doi.org/10.1186/s41239-018-0093-2.

Nelson, M. 2017. "The Digital Transformation of HE." Presented at the
Plenary Keynote Session, 2017 EMOOCS Conference. (Video.) https://
www.youtube.com/watch?v=0VoxL6lIX6g.

Newman, T., and H. Beetham. 2017. *Student Digital Experience Tracker
2017: The Voice of 22000 UK Learners.* London: JISC. http://repository
.jisc.ac.uk/6662/1/Jiscdigitalstudenttracker2017.pdf.

Newton, C. 2016. "Can AI Fix Education? We Asked Bill Gates." *Verge*, April
25. https://www.theverge.com/2016/4/25/11492102/bill-gates-interview
-education-software-artificial-intelligence.

Noble, D. 1998. "Digital Diploma Mills: The Automation of Higher Education." *First Monday* 3, no. 1. https://firstmonday.org/ojs/index.php/fm/
article/view/569/490.

Noble, S. U. 2018. *Algorithms of Oppression: How Search Engines Reinforce
Racism.* New York: New York University Press.

OECD. 2018. *Education at a Glance 2018.* Paris: OECD.

OER World Map. n.d. Accessed August 16, 2019, at https://oerworldmap
.org/.

Oliver, M. 2015. "From Openness to Permeability: Reframing Open
Education in Terms of Positive Liberty in the Enactment of Academic
Practices." *Learning, Media and Technology* 40, no. 3: 365–384. https://
doi.org/10.1080/17439884.2015.1029940.

Olson, P. 2018. "Building Brains: How Pearson Plans to Automate
Education with AI." *Forbes*, August 29. https://www.forbes.com/sites/
parmyolson/2018/08/29/pearson-education-ai/.

Olssen, M., and M. A. Peters. 2005. "Neoliberalism, Higher Education
and the Knowledge Economy: From the Free Market to Knowledge

Capitalism." *Journal of Education Policy* 20, no. 3: 313–345. https://doi.org/10.1080/02680930500108718.

O'Neil, C. 2016. *Weapons of Math Destruction: How Big Data Increases Inequality and Threatens Democracy*. London: Penguin.

O'Neill, O. 2002. "A Question of Trust." Accessed November 17, 2019, at http://www.bbc.co.uk/radio4/reith2002/.

Ong, W. 1960. "Wired for Sound: Teaching, Communications and Technological Culture." *College English* 21, no. 5: 245–251. https://doi.org/10.2307/373335.

Online Course Report. 2017. *The 50 Most Popular MOOCs of All Time*. https://www.onlinecoursereport.com/the-50-most-popular-moocs-of-all-time/.

OnTask. 2019. Accessed March 5, 2020, at https://www.ontasklearning.org/.

Open Education Consortium. 2018. "OEC Announces the 2018 Winners of Open Resources, Tools and Practices for Open Education." March 21. http://www.oeconsortium.org/2018/03/oec-announces-the-2018-oe-award-winners-of-open-resources-tools-practices/.

O'Shea C., and M. Dozier. 2014. "That Ever-Ephemeral Sense of 'Being Somewhere': Reflections on a Dissertation Festival in Second Life." In *Teaching and Learning in Virtual Worlds*, edited by C. DeCoursey and S. Garrett, 159–189. Oxford: Inter-Disciplinary Press.

O'Shea, C., and T. Fawns. 2014. "Disruptions and Dialogues: Supporting Collaborative Connoisseurship in Digital Environments." In *Advances and Innovations in University Assessment and Feedback*, edited by C. Kreber, C. Anderson, N. Entwistle, and J. McArthur, 259–273. Edinburgh: Edinburgh University Press.

Papamitsiou, Z., and A. A. Economides. 2014. "Temporal Learning Analytics for Adaptive Assessment." *Journal of Learning Analytics* 1, no. 3: 165–168.

Pappano, L. 2012. *The Year of the MOOC* (blog). http://www.nytimes.com/2012/11/04/education/edlife/massive-open-online-courses-are-multiplying-at-a-rapid-pace.html.

Pedersen, H. 2015. "Education and Posthumanism." *Critical Posthumanities: Genealogy of the Posthuman.* http://criticalposthumanism.net/genealogy/education/.

Penketh, C., and C. Beaumont. 2014. "'Turnitin Said It Wasn't Happy': Can the Regulatory Discourse of Plagiarism Detection Operate as a Change Artefact for Writing Development?" *Innovations in Education and Teaching International* 51, no. 1: 95–104. https://doi.org/10.1080/14703 297.2013.796721.

Perna, L., A. Ruby, R. Boruch, N. Wang, J. Scull, C. Evans, and S. Ahmad. 2013. "The Life Cycle of a Million MOOC Users." Paper presented at the MOOC Research Initiative Conference, Arlington, TX, December 5. http://www.gse.upenn.edu/pdf/ahead/perna_ruby_boruch_moocs_dec2013.pdf.

Perrotta, C., and B. Williamson. 2018. "The Social Life of Learning Analytics: Cluster Analysis and the 'Performance' of Algorithmic Education." *Learning, Media and Technology* 43, no. 1: 3–16. https://doi.org/10.1080/17439884.2016.1182927.

Phan, L. H. 2014. "The Politics of Naming: Critiquing 'Learner-Centred' and 'Teacher as Facilitator' in English Language and Humanities Classrooms." *Asia-Pacific Journal of Teacher Education* 42, no. 4: 392–405. https://doi.org/0.1080/1359866X.2014.956048.

Phillips, A. 2018. "The Future of AI and Education." *Inside Big Data*, May 18. https://insidebigdata.com/2018/05/13/future-ai-education/.

Poster, M. 2001. *What's the Matter with the Internet?* Minneapolis: University of Minnesota Press.

Prensky, M. 2001a. "Digital Natives, Digital Immigrants." *On the Horizon* 9, no. 5.

Prensky, M. 2001b. "Digital Natives, Digital Immigrants, Part II: Do They Really Think Differently?" *On the Horizon* 9, no. 6.

Prinsloo, P. 2016. "Decolonising the Collection, Analyses and Use of Student Data: A Tentative Exploration/Proposal." *Open Distance Teaching and Learning* (blog). https://opendistanceteachingandlearning.wordpress.com/2016/11/14/decolonising-the-collection-analyses-and-use-of-student-data-a-tentative-explorationproposal/.

Prinsloo, P., and S. Slade. 2016. "Student Vulnerability, Agency, and Learning Analytics: An Exploration." *Journal of Learning Analytics* 13, no. 1: 159–182.

Quinlan, K. 2016. "How Emotion Matters in Teaching and Learning in Four Key Relationships in Higher Education." *College Teaching* 64, no. 3: 102–111. https://doi.org/10.1080/87567555.2015.1088818.

Radcliffe, S. A. 2017. "Geography and Indigeneity I: Indigeneity, Coloniality and Knowledge." *Progress in Human Geography* 41, no. 2: 220–229.

Ramachandran, V. S. 2012. *The Tell-Tale Brain: Unlocking the Mystery of Human Nature*. London: Windmill.

Reuters. 2019. "Artificial Intelligence in Education Market 2019: Emerging Technologies, Global Trends, Segments, Competitive Landscape and Growth by Forecast to 2023." Press release, June 11. https://www.reuters.com/brandfeatures/venture-capital/article?id=119017.

Richardson, I. 2007. "Pocket Technospaces: The Bodily Incorporation of Mobile Media." *Continuum: Journal of Media and Cultural Studies* 21, no. 2: 205–215.

Rivera-Velez, L. M., and F. Thibault. 2015. "Public Digital Policies in Higher Education—a Comparative Survey between Spain, France, Italy and the United Kingdom." http://www.dtransform.eu/wp-content/uploads/2016/01/01.A1Eng.pdf.

Robertson, S. L., and K. Olds. 2018. "Locating Universities in a Globalising World." In *Higher Education Strategy and Planning. A Professional Guide*, edited by T. Strike, 13–29. Abingdon: Routledge.

Ross, J. 2016. "Speculative Method in Digital Education Research." *Learning, Media and Technology* 42, no 2: 214–229. https://doi.org/10.1080/17439884.2016.1160927.

Ross, J., and Collier, A. 2016. "Complexity, Mess, and Not-Yetness: Teaching Online with Emerging Technologies." In *Emergence and Innovation in Digital Learning*, edited by G. Veletsianos, 17–33. Edmonton: Athabasca University Press.

Ross, J., and P. Sheail. 2017. "The 'Campus Imaginary': Online Students' Experience of the Master's Dissertation at a Distance." *Teaching in Higher Education* 22, no. 7: 839–854. https://doi.org/10.1080/13562517.2017.1319809.

Rushkoff, D. 1994. *Media Virus: Hidden Agendas in Popular Culture.* New York: Ballantine.

Rushkoff, D. 1996. *Playing the Future: How Kids' Culture Can Teach Us to Thrive in an Age of Chaos.* New York: HarperCollins.

Ryan, M. 2010. "Can You Afford Not to Go to University?" London: BBC. http://news.bbc.co.uk/1/hi/education/8556307.stm.

Sampson, T. D., S. Maddison, and D. Ellis, eds. 2018. *Affect and Social Media: Emotion, Mediation, Anxiety and Contagion.* London: Rowman and Littlefield International.

Schaberg, C. 2018. "Why I Won't Teach Online." *Inside Higher Education*, March 7. https://www.insidehighered.com/digital-learning/views/2018/03/07/professor-explains-why-he-wont-teach-online-opinion.

Schaub, A., R. Bazin, O. Hasan, and L. Brunie. 2016. "A Trustless Privacy-Preserving Reputation System." In *ICT Systems Security and Privacy Protection*, edited by J.-H. Hoepman and S. Katzenbeisser, 398–411. Cham: Springer. https://doi.org/10.1007/978-3-319-33630-5_27.

Schwab, K. 2016. *The Fourth Industrial Revolution.* New York: Crown Business.

Selby, M., and D. Kirk. 2015. "Experiential Manufacturing: The Earthquake Shelf." In *Proceedings of the 2nd Biennial Research Through Design Conference*, art. 17. https://doi.org/10.6084/m9.figshare.1327994.

Selingo, J. J. 2015. "Grade Point: What's the Purpose of College: A Job or an Education?" *Washington Post*, February 2. https://www.washingtonpost.com/news/grade-point/wp/2015/02/02/whats-the-purpose-of-college-a-job-or-an-education.

Selwyn, N. 2009a. "The Digital Native: Myth and Reality." *Aslib Proceedings: New Information Perspectives* 61, no. 4: 364–379. https://doi.org/10.1108/00012530910973776.

Selwyn, N. 2009b. "The 'New' Connectivities of Digital Education." In *The Routledge International Handbook of the Sociology of Education*, edited by M. W. Apple, S. J. Ball, and L. A. Gandin, 90–98. London: Routledge. https://doi.org/10.4324/9780203863701.ch8.

Selwyn, N. 2014. *Digital Technology and the Contemporary University: Degrees of Digitization*. Abingdon: Routledge.

Sennett, R. 2006. *The Culture of the New Capitalism*. London: Yale University Press.

Shah, D. 2018a. "By the Numbers: MOOCS in 2018." *Class Central*. https://www.classcentral.com/report/mooc-stats-2018/.

Shah, D. 2018b. "MasterTrack: Coursera's Newest Micro-Credential. Class Central." https://www.class-central.com/report/mastertrack-coursera/.

Sharmer, O. 2017. "MOOC 4.0: The Next Revolution in Learning and Leadership." *Huffington Post*. https://www.huffingtonpost.com/entry/mooc-40-the-next-revoluti_b_7209606.html.

Sheail, P. 2015. "The Motif of Meeting in Digital Education." *TechTrends* 59, no. 1: 37–43.

Sheail, P. 2018. "The Digital University and the Shifting Time-Space of the Campus." *Learning, Media and Technology* 43, no. 1: 56–69. https://doi.org/10.1080/17439884.2017.1387139.

Sheller, M., and J. Urry, J. 2006. "The New Mobilities Paradigm." *Environment and Planning A: Economy and Space* 38, no. 2: 207–226. https://doi.org/10.1068/a37268.

Shin, D.S., and T. Cimasko. 2008. "Multimodal Composition in a College ESL Class: New Tools, Traditional Norms." *Computers and Composition* 25, no. 4: 376–395. https://doi.org/10.1016/j.compcom.2008.07.001.

Silva, A. de Souza e, and J. Frith. 2010. "Locational Privacy in Public Spaces: Media Discourses on Location-Aware Mobile Technologies." *Communication, Culture and Critique* 3, no. 4: 503–525.

Simons, M, and J. Masschelein. 2008. "The Governmentalization of Learning and the Assemblage of a Learning Apparatus." *Educational Theory* 58, no. 4: 391–415. https://doi.org/10.1111/j.1741-5446.2008.00296.x.

Simpson, O. 2013. "Student Retention in Distance Education: Are We Failing Our Students?" *Open Learning* 28, no. 2: 105–119. https://doi.org/10.1080/02680513.2013.847363.

Sin, C., O. Tavares, and A. Amaral. 2017. "Accepting Employability as a Purpose of Higher Education? Academics' Perceptions and Practices." *Studies in Higher Education* 44, no 6: 920–931. https://doi.org/10.1080/03075079.2017.1402174.

Singh, G., and G. Hardaker. 2017. "Change Levers for Unifying Top-Down and Bottom-Up Approaches to the Adoption and Diffusion of E-Learning in Higher Education." *Teaching in Higher Education* 22, no. 6: 736–748. https://doi.org/10.1080/13562517.2017.1289508.

Snaza, N. 2014. "Toward a Genealogy of Educational Humanism." In *Posthumanism and Educational Research,* edited by N. Snaza and J. Weaver, 17–29. New York: Routledge.

SOLAR: Society for Learning Analytics Research. Accessed August 16, 2019, at https://solaresearch.org/.

Sørensen, E. 2009. *The Materiality of Learning: Technology and Knowledge in Educational Practice.* New York: Cambridge University Press.

Srnicek, N. 2017. *Platform Capitalism.* Cambridge UK: Polity Press.

Stewart, B. 2013. "Massiveness + Openness = New Literacies of Participation?" *MERLOT Journal of Online Learning and Technology* 9, no. 2: 228–238.

Stewart, B. 2015. "Open to Influence: What Counts as Academic Influence in Scholarly Networked Twitter Participation." *Learning, Media and Technology* 40, no. 3: 287–309. https://doi.org/10.1080/17439884.2015.1015547.

Stone, A. R. 1991. "Will the Real Body Please Stand Up?" In *Cyberspace: First Steps,* edited by M. Benedikt, 81–118. Cambridge, MA: MIT Press.

Striphas, T. 2015. "Algorithmic Culture." *European Journal of Cultural Studies* 18, no. 4–5: 395–412. https://doi.org/10.1177/1367549415577392.

Suppes, P. 1966. "The Uses of Computers in Education." *Scientific American* 215, no. 2: 206–220.

Swartz, R., M. Ivancheva, L. Czerniewicz, and N. Morris. 2018. "Between a Rock and a Hard Place: Dilemmas regarding the Purpose of Public Universities in South Africa." *Higher Education* 77, no. 4: 567–583. https://doi.org/10.1007/s10734-018-0291-9.

Swinnerton, B., M. Ivancheva, T. Coop, C. Perotta, N. Morris, R. Swartz, L. Czerniewicz, S. Cliff, and S. Walji, 2018. "The Unbundled University: Researching Emerging Models in an Unequal Landscape. Preliminary Findings from Fieldwork in South Africa." In *Proceedings of the 11th International Conference on Networked Learning 2018*, edited by M. Bajić, N. B. Dohn, M. de Laat, P. Jandrić, and T. Ryberg, 218–226. Zagreb: Zagreb University of Applied Sciences.

Tams, S., and M. B. Arthur. 2010. "New Directions for Boundaryless Careers: Agency and Interdependence in a Changing World." *Journal of Organizational Behavior* 31, no. 5: 629–646. https://doi.org/10.1002/job.712.

Tandoc, E. C., Jr., P. Ferrucci, and M. Duffy. 2015. "Facebook Use, Envy, and Depression among College Students: Is Facebooking Depressing?" *Computers in Human Behavior* 43:139–146. https://doi.org/10.1016/j.chb.2014.10.053.

Taylor, C. A. 2016. "Edu-crafting a Cacophonous Ecology: Posthumanist Research Practices for Education." In *Posthuman Research Practices in Education*, edited by C. A. Taylor and C. Hughes, 5–24. London: Palgrave Macmillan UK.

Taylor, J. C. 2011. "The OER University: From Logic Model to Action Plan." Open planning meeting for the OER for Assessment and Credit for Students Project, February 23, Dunedin, New Zealand. http://wikieducator.org/OER_for_Assessment_and_Credit_for_Students/Meeting_Summary_-_23_Feb_2011.

Townley, C., and M. Parsell. 2004. "Technology and Academic Virtue: Student Plagiarism Through the Looking Glass." *Ethics and Information Technology* 6, no. 4: 271–277. https://doi.org/10.1007/s10676-005-5606-8.

Tschannen-Moran, M., and W. Hoy. 1998. "Trust in Schools: A Conceptual and Empirical Analysis." *Journal of Educational Administration* 36, no. 4: 334–352. https://doi.org/10.1108/09578239810211518.

Tsai, Y. S., and D. Gašević. 2017. "Learning Analytics in Higher Education-Challenges and Policies: A Review of Eight Learning Analytics Policies." In *Proceedings of the Seventh International Learning Analytics and Knowledge Conference*, 233–242. New York: ACM.

Turner, C. 2018. "Schools Should Teach Children Resilience to Help Them in the Workplace, New Education Secretary Says." *Telegraph*, January 22. http://www.telegraph.co.uk/education/2018/01/22/schools-should-teach-children-resilience-help-workplace-new/.

Turnitin n.d. Accessed August 16, 2019, at https://www.turnitin.com/divisions/higher-education.

Universities UK. 2016. "Analytics in Higher Education." Accessed March 13, 2020, at https://www.universitiesuk.ac.uk/policy-and-analysis/reports/Pages/analytics-in-higher-education.aspx.

University of California Santa Barbara. n.d. "Questions to Be Addressed in Proposals for First-Time Offering of Online Courses." Accessed August 16, 2019, at https://senate.ucsb.edu/resources.for.department.faculty.and.staff/courses.and.instruction/Supplemental.Materials.for.Review.of.New.Online.Courses.pdf.

Urry, J. 2007. *Mobilities*. Cambridge: Polity Press.

Urry, J. 2016. *What Is the Future?* Cambridge: Polity Press.

Usher, R., and R. Edwards. 1994. *Postmodernism and Education: Different Voices, Different Worlds*. London: Routledge.

Vaidhyanathan, S. 2018. *Antisocial Media: How Facebook Disconnects Us and Undermines Democracy*. Oxford: Oxford University Press.

van der Velden, M. 2009. "Design for a Common World: On Ethical Agency and Cognitive Justice." *Ethics and Information Technology* 11, no. 1: 37–47. https://doi.org/10.1007/s10676-008-9178-2.

van Doorn, N. 2011. "Digital Spaces, Material Traces: How Matter Comes to Matter in Online Performances of Gender, Sexuality and Embodiment." *Media, Culture and Society* 33, no. 4: 531–547. https://doi.org/10.1177/0163443711398692.

Veletsianos, G. 2010. *Emerging Technologies in Distance Education*. Athabasca: Athabasca University Press.

Veletsianos, G., and R. Moe. 2017. "The Rise of Educational Technology as a Sociocultural and Ideological Phenomenon." *Educause Review* (April). http://er.educause.edu/articles/2017/4/the-rise-of-educational -technology-as-a-sociocultural-and-ideological-phenomenon.

Vie, S. 2013. "A Pedagogy of Resistance toward Plagiarism Detection Technologies." *Computers and Composition* 30, no. 1: 3–15. https://doi.org/ 10.1016/j.compcom.2013.01.002.

von Radowitz, J. 2017. "Intelligent Machines Will Replace Teachers within 10 Years, Leading Public School Headteacher Predicts." *Independent*. https://www.independent.co.uk/news/education/education-news/ intelligent-machines-replace-teachers-classroom-10-years-ai-robots-sir -anthony-sheldon-wellington-a7939931.html.

Wajcman, J. 2015. *Pressed for Time: The Acceleration of Life in Digital Capitalism*. Chicago: University of Chicago Press.

Walsh, L. 2015. "The Tail Wagging the Dog? Emergent Trends and Drivers of International Digital Education." In *The Sage Handbook of Research in International Education*, 2nd ed., edited by M. Hayden, J. Levy, and J. Thompson, 233–245. London: Sage.

Warner, J. 2018. "Guest Post: A Season of Strikes." *Inside Higher Ed* (blog). http://www.insidehighered.com/blogs/just-visiting/guest-post-season -strikes.

Watters, A. 2015. "A History of MOOCs: Mythology and Wikiality." Hack Education. http://hackeducation.com/2015/04/12/wikiality.

Wetherell, M. 2012. *Affect and Emotion: A New Social Science Understanding*. London: Sage.

Wicklow, K. 2017. "For Accelerated Degrees, Do We Feel the Need for Speed?" *WonkHE* (blog), December 11. https://wonkhe.com/blogs/for -accelerated-degrees-do-we-feel-the-need-for-speed/.

Wiley, D. 2014. "The Access Compromise and the 5th R." *Opencontent .org* (blog). https://opencontent.org/blog/archives/3221.

Williamson, B. 2014. "Organizing Algorithms, Calculated Publics in Digitally-Mediated Education." DML central. http://dmlcentral.net/ organizing-algorithms-calculated-publics-in-digitally-mediated-education/.

Williamson, B. 2015. "Governing Software: Networks, Databases and Algorithmic Power in the Digital Governance of Public Education." *Learning, Media and Technology* 40, no. 1: 83–105. https://doi.org/10.1080/17439884.2014.924527.

Williamson, B. 2017. *Big Data in Education: The Digital Future of Learning, Policy and Practice.* London: Sage.

Williamson, B. 2019a. "Policy Networks, Performance Metrics and Platform Markets: Charting the Expanding Data Infrastructure of Higher Education." *British Journal of Educational Technology* 50:2794–2809. https://doi.org/10.1111/bjet.12849.

Williamson, B. 2019b. "Brain Data: Scanning, Scraping and Sculpting the Plastic Learning Brain through Neurotechnology." *Postdigital Science and Education* 1:65–86. https://doi.org/10.1007/s42438-018-0008-5.

Winn, M. 1977. *The Plug-In Drug: Television, Children, and the Family.* New York: Viking Penguin.

World Bank Institute. 2009. "Measuring Knowledge in the World's Economies. Knowledge for Development Program, 1–12." http://siteresources.worldbank.org/INTUNIKAM/Resources/KAM_v4.pdf.

Wright, R. 2001. *Nonzero: History, Evolution and Human Cooperation.* London: Abacus.

Wyatt, S. 2008. "Technological Determinism Is Dead; Long Live Technological Determinism." In *The Handbook of Science and Technology Studies*, 3rd ed., edited by E. Hackett, O. Amsterdamska, M. Lynch, and J. Wajcman, 165–180. Cambridge, MA: MIT Press.

Year of Open. 2018. "What Is the Year of Open 2018?" Accessed August 16, 2019, at https://www.yearofopen.org/what-is-the-year-of-open/.

Youmans, R. J. 2011. "Does the Adoption of Plagiarism-Detection Software in Higher Education Reduce Plagiarism?" *Studies in Higher Education* 36, no. 7: 749–761. https://doi.org/10.1080/03075079.2010.523457.

Zgaga, P. 2009. "Higher Education and Citizenship: 'The Full Range of Purposes.'" *European Educational Research Journal* 8, no. 2: 175–188. https://doi.org/10.2304/eerj.2009.8.2.175.

Ziewitz, M. 2015. "Governing Algorithms: Myth, Mess, and Methods." *Science, Technology and Human Values* 41, no. 1: 3–16. https://doi.org/10.1177/0162243915608948.

Zuboff, S. 2015. "Big Other: Surveillance Capitalism and the Prospects of an Information Civilization." *Journal of Information Technology* 30:75–89.

Zwagerman, S. 2008. "The Scarlet P: Plagiarism, Panopticism, and the Rhetoric of Academic Integrity." *College Composition and Communication* 59, no. 4: 676–710.

INDEX